$3

TEACHERS OF DESTRUCTION

Their Plans for a Socialist Revolution

AN EYEWITNESS ACCOUNT

by

ALICE WIDENER

Epilogue

by

J. EDGAR HOOVER

Published by

THE CITIZENS EVALUATION INSTITUTE

To F.L.S. Wood

ACKNOWLEDGMENT

Gratefully, I wish to thank my assistant, Joseph Falzon, and Newton H. Fulbright and Earl B. Dunckel for their constructive criticism, editorial help and encouragement in my work.

TABLE OF CONTENTS

THE AUTHOR

Alice Widener, internationally known syndicated columnist, analyst, lecturer and publisher of *U.S.A. Magazine,* is described by *Barron's National Business & Financial Weekly* as "an authority on the Old and New Left." She has won many honors, including the National Recognition Award (1968) from Freedoms Foundation at Valley Forge, and Citation of Merit (1969) highest award of the American Vocational Association, Washington, D.C.

In 1967, *Editor & Publisher,* top professional journal of the publishing world, described Mrs. Widener as a writer and analyst with "an outstanding record for discerning trends and reporting them, who is often ahead of others in interpreting developments, gets straight facts and logically and simply presents the A.B.C.'s."

The reliability of her first-hand research and reporting for this study, backed by documents in her library from as early as 1905, have attracted to her desk a flow of source material and information from students and faculty members at leading schools and universities.

Almost single-handed she has covered and reported on the meetings of the Socialist Scholars since 1965. She has analyzed their plans for destruction and observed the growing arrogance of their techniques and the alarming results.

The high esteem in which her work is held can be judged by the endorsements from those who know her work.

J. Edgar Hoover says: *"I have noted with a great deal of interest your writings . . . and hope that you will continue your good work, particularly in alerting the American public to the dangers of the Communist menace."*

Taylor Caldwell says, *"U.S.A. does not come often enough. It is the journal of educated and reasonable people desperately concerned with the state of their country's future."*

Mortality In Media News Letter reports, *". . . She is courageous; she is deeply concerned about moral deterioration in the nation. . ."*

Maurice B. Mitchell, Chancellor, University of Denver, says: *Alice Widener emerges as the only on-the-scene reporter of the underground planning that produced campus violence in America and laid the foundation for a domestic revolution.*

"The reports . . . are the blunt, factual and significant notes of a great journalist. They are must reading for the survivors of the future."

INTRODUCTION

WHAT DO MARXIST teachers of destruction seek to construct?

"A socialist society," they say.

Does anyone in this day and age still believe that the Marxists and their well-trained pupils don't mean what they say?

In February 1968, I reported on a regional meeting held in the subcellar of Weinstein Hall at New York University by Students for a Democratic Society. In an article entitled "Subcellar Student Subversion" for my own *U.S.A. Magazine*, I revealed that they planned to lead a violent student rebellion on American campuses during the ten days April 21— April 30, 1968. When the article appeared in *Barron's National Business and Financial Weekly*, March 11, it bore the more specific and graphic title "Ten Days in April."

"At New York University, over the weekend of February 10-11, 1968," I reported, "Students for a Democratic Society held a regional conference to help plan SDS' program for ten days of violence and disruption in our American communities during next April 21—April 30. Steven Halliwell of SDS at Columbia University was a main speaker. He urged his listeners to become like the revolutionary students at universities in Russia during the 'pre-Leninist period.' An overall theme of SDS today is that 1968 can be 'the 1905' of the American revolution. What the radical students mean is that they know they cannot bring down the American government as soon as 1968, but they expect that their violent revolutionary activities, even though put down this year, will force the police to use force against the students, and thus create resentment against our government in the same manner as the unsuccessful Marxist-inspired Russian revolution of 1905 did against the Czarist regime."

My article on the SDS meeting at Weinstein Hall, New York University, February 1968, concluded with the following two paragraphs:

"If Students for a Democratic Society members are permitted to carry out their planned ten-day program of violent resistance in April, with accompanying bloodshed, then an outraged and angry American public will fix the blame where it belongs, on university trustees, directors and administrators. They should act now and announce that any student taking part in any illegal activity will be instantly expelled."

"The recent SDS regional conference at New York University was a disgrace to that institution and an outrage against the citizenry. From coast to coast, Americans should demand that university administrators get control over their own institutions or get out. Otherwise, student subversion, abetted in some instances by faculty members, can eventually accomplish its aim and bring down our free American university system and free U.S. Government."

For a few weeks after publication, my article about what SDS planned in February for April suffered from an extensive credibility gap. Geoffrey Kent, a student reporter for the New York University campus newspaper, *Washington Square Journal*, wrote in the March 21 issue that in response to letters of inquiry to the N.Y.U. administration from readers of the article across the country, asking how N.Y.U. could permit such a meeting on campus, Chancellor Allan M. Cartter said, "We don't intend to supervise duly constituted groups. If they really were engaging in violent activities, we would take a different position." Mr. Kent quoted N.Y.U. Vice Chancellor Harold B. Whiteman as saying, "The lady was over-reacting, and hadn't been around students and didn't know how they talked." Chancellor Whiteman further declared that the SDS subcellar Weinstein Hall meeting was "not very significant compared to what else is going on around the country and around the world."

On April 23, 1968—ten weeks after the SDS planning session in February at Weinstein Hall—the riotous SDS-led rebellion at Columbia University took place right on schedule and became headline news in our country and around the world!

Yet in most upper-echelon academic administrative circles there had been little credence in my warning of what was about to take place, and there also was considerable press skepticism about it.

In mid-afternoon, April 22, 1968, I received a long distance telephone call from the editorial-page editor of a newspaper carrying my thrice-weekly column on national and international affairs.

"Mrs. Widener," he said abruptly, without a friendly or even polite greeting, "do you know what day this is?"

Thinking he might be as wholly absorbed as I while working, or that his desk might be as disorderly as mine, I hastily fumbled among papers near my typewriter to dig out a calendar.

"It's April 22nd," I said, afraid of having somehow missed a deadline.

"Right! And aren't you ashamed of yourself? You wrote that piece in *Barron's* about some kind of violent campus rebellion beginning the 21st, and you spread rumors around the country about what radical students are going to do, and here it is the 22nd and everything is quiet as can be. You said it would happen in the ten days April 21—April 30. I repeat, aren't you ashamed of yourself?"

I kept silent.

"Haven't you anything to say?" demanded the editor. "Haven't you anything at all to say?"

For a moment I hesitated, subduing my feelings. "Thank you for calling," I said. "All I have to say is—we'll see."

The remainder of my day was spent at work until very late at night.

Sound asleep early next morning, I was awakened by a phone call. An unfamiliar male voice said courteously, "I'm sorry to call so early. This is Douglas Lovelace, chief, New York Bureau, Associated Press."

Mr. Lovelace said he'd like to send a messenger to my office to pick up a copy of the *Barron's* article "Ten Days in April" and also any copies I could furnish of my past articles on the Socialist Scholars Conference organization and on Students for a Democratic Society. "I seem to remember a piece of yours about a Socialist Scholars meeting at Columbia as far back as 1965," he added.

I said my assistant would be glad to collect the pieces for him. "What's up?" I inquired, and asked Mr. Lovelace why he needed the material in such a hurry.

"All hell has broken loose at Columbia University," came the grim reply. "Unfortunately, you were right. I'd like your pieces for research purposes. You're the one in the press who's been following what faculty and student radicals are doing."

THE CLEVER, SUSTAINED ASSAULT

Sad to say, Mr. Lovelace was right. How much better it would have been for our country if other writers and reporters in the big press had attended the meetings held by radical Leftist students and teachers, meetings that were openly announced in the radical press, such as the *Militant*, *Guardian*, Communist *Daily World* and in the obscene "underground" press. Perhaps the television, radio and newspaper reporters were absent because their assignment editors, like the Chancellor and Vice Chancellor of New York University, held the opinion that the radicals were too few in number for their plotting and planning to be very significant in comparison to what else was going on around our country and the world.

That is what complacent, apathetic or uninformed people believed in 1848 when Karl Marx called for a new "scientific society" and a new "scientific man," and wrote the "Communist Manifesto" with Frederick Engels. In it, they penned a total indictment of the history of mankind and singled out "the bourgeoisie," that is, the property-owning middle class, as a collective devil in human society. Marx and Engels also singled out the "proletariat," that is, the industrial factory workers, as a class destined to set up a world socialist dictatorship led by a "vanguard," the Communist Party elite. But nowhere in the entire literature of the Left since 1848, including the twentieth century writings of Lenin, Stalin, Trotsky and Mao Tse-tung, and of Professor Herbert Marcuse and "existentialist" Jean Paul Sartre, is there any clear picture of what life in a Socialist or Communist society would be like and of precisely how it would be run.

All Marxist writings are merciless indictments of past and present human society, like briefs prepared by an unfair prosecutor seeking indictment of an accused person whether guilty or innocent.

Today in our country, all Communists and Marxists, including the members of the Socialist Scholars Conference, a tax-exempt membership organization founded in 1965, are teachers of destruction, not peaceful reformers working for the gradual improvement of our society. They instruct their pupils to be against the entire past and existing traditional social and political order of things.

In May 1970, at the United States Military Academy at West Point, Vice President Agnew told the graduating class of cadets, "These are years of great national confusion, much of it contrived confusion brought about by a clever, sustained assault on America's systems and institutions."

Shortly thereafter, eleven Regents Professors on the faculty of the University of Minnesota went to Washington, D.C. to see the Vice President and express their displeasure over his remarks at West Point. They asked him to moderate his public rhetoric, claiming that it is "driving moderates into the arms of extremists" on and off campus.

There is no public record, however, that at any time during the last five years any group of faculty members at the University of Minnesota or any other university in our country went to Washington, or to New York City, or to any campus to ask a leading Socialist Scholar to moderate his rhetoric, or to ask that any leading book publisher moderate the rhetoric in any of the violently revolutionary Marxist propaganda tracts issued by him.

Yet ever since September 1965, I have reported in *U.S.A. Magazine*, in my newspaper columns and on the front page of *Barron's* the full story of the Socialist Scholars' and their pupils' clever and sustained assault on America's systems and institutions, an assault expressed in rhetoric more brutal and extreme than that in Hitler's *Mein Kampf.*

In September 1965, Socialist Scholar Herbert Aptheker, of the Communist Party, U.S.A., described the tragic riots in Watts, Los Angeles, as "glorious."

In September 1966, Socialist Scholar Professor Herbert Marcuse of the University of California at San Diego declared that "the Marxian idea of socialism is not radical enough. We must develop the moral-sexual rebellion of the youth."

In September 1967, Socialist Scholar Dr. Owen Lattimore accused the United States of seeking to make Asia "the privileged reserve of white men," and Socialist Scholar panelist Ivanhoe Donaldson said from the dais, "The struggle of the [nineteen] sixties isn't the ballot or having jobs—it is a physical struggle. Our position is—tear it down because we don't want to be a part of it!"

In September 1968, the Socialist Scholars' guest of honor, Dr. Ernest Mandel, Belgian Marxist editor of the radical journal *La Gauche*, declared, "Students are the detonators in the formula for triggering off a social explosion creating a revolutionary situation."

In September 1969, Socialist Scholar Martin Jay, teaching fellow, Harvard University, explained, "Our movement is a movement which, in effect, is a total break with America."

In May 1970, publisher Simon & Schuster issued for distribution on newsstands throughout our nation the vile paperback book "Do It!" by Jerry Rubin, a member of the Chicago Conspiracy Seven who took part in the violent demonstrations during the 1968 Democratic National Convention. Rubin has urged our youth, "Kill your parents!"

Has any distinguished academic group issued a collective public protest against such rhetoric, which not only drives many young moderates and dupes into the arms of extremists but also causes violence that drives students, policemen, firemen, civic officials and innocent bystanders into hospitals and, in some cases, into early graves?

Did any distinguished academic group journey to Chicago in 1966 to ask Dr. Robert Havighurst, professor of education at the University of Chicago, why he acted as co-chairman of the organizing conference of the Committee for Independent Political Action (CIPA), a Marxist and Communist group, at which Nahaz Rogers, a black militant, said, "We are not here to do good. We are here to seize power. Don't ask us what we'll do with it when we get it. First we have to get it. The democratic process is a great thing, *but you don't come to the democratic process democratically.*"

Why didn't a distinguished academic group journey to the West Coast to ask Professor Herbert Marcuse of the University of California at San Diego to moderate his Marxist rhetoric? It won him worldwide recognition as the "intellectual mentor" of "Red" Rudi Dutschke, who in 1967 led the bloody student riots in West Berlin, and of "Red" Danny Cohn-Bendit, who led violent students in the 1968 May-June rebellion in France that nearly wrecked the entire economic and political structure of that country.

"We are not here to do good. We are here to seize power. Don't ask us what we'll do with it when we get it. First we have to get it."

That is what "Red" Rudi Dutschke and "Red" Danny Cohn-Bendit said; and that is what Mark Rudd of the revolutionary communist Students for a Democratic Society said when he led the violent rebellion at Columbia University in April 1968.

THE SOCIALIST STRATEGY

In their efforts to get power, radical Marxists use the technique of making demands that cannot be granted by an institution without its administrators' agreeing to its destruction. "We use the technique of demands, always pushing and pushing on through demands, to an end where they have to give in or fight against the revolution," said Dave Gilbert, a graduate student at the New School for Social Research in Manhattan, who addressed the SDS Radical Education Project regional conference at Princeton University, February 1967.

Three years later, the Socialist Scholars, a radical Marxist brain trust in our country, held their sixth annual conference in June 1970 on the premises of a New York City public school. There they circulated a position paper entitled "Towards a Socialist Strategy for the United States." Written by so-called "New Left" authors Frank Brodhead, Edward Greer, Amy Kesselman, Karl Klare and Ruth Meyerowitz, the paper declares, "The creation of a truly socialist society requires a redefinition of man as well as a new model of civilization." They go on to say (as does every radical Socialist in every free country today), "Although we can begin to develop the outline of socialist relationships now, we can only complete the construction of a socialist society after power has been taken from those who live off, profit from and have an interest in maintaining the capitalist system."

To date, there is no great literary work of fiction or non-fiction written by a Marxist to picture in detail the ideal Marxian society in a new model of civilization. The greatest fictional critique of life in such an imaginary future society is *1984* by George Orwell. Such literary fictional masterpieces as *Darkness at Noon* by Arthur Koestler, *Fall of the Titan* by Igor Gouzenko, and *Atlas Shrugged* by Ayn Rand depict the actual horrors of life under dictators seeking to establish a Marxian society without private, free and competitive enterprise.

The 1970 position paper "Towards a Socialist Strategy for the United States" by the five "New Left" authors declares that the socialists' first strategic aim is "to launch the social and cultural revolution on all fronts. This means desanctifying and putting into crisis all capitalist institutions and social relationships." Openly, authors Brodhead, Greer, Kesselman, Klare and Meyerowitz call for creation in our country of a "resistance culture."

Their second strategic aim is "seizure of state power," and they declare, as did Marx and Lenin, "As a last resort, and often sooner, the capitalist class will use its control of the state apparatus to suppress revolutionary activity. Thus, to carry through the revolution, it will be necessary to seize and dismantle the bourgeois state apparatus and to replace it by political forms which represent the working class."

YEARS OF SOCIALIST TRAINING

Resistance culture was taught to some of our youth by socialist teachers from the early days of the first Marxist groups in our country during the latter part of the nineteenth century on into the early part of our century. The violently radical Leftist students of today did not spring out of the nowhere into the here; they were trained up in the way the Marxist academicians and intellectuals thought they should go.

In the first decade of our century, Marxists set up special schools of "social science" and established in 1905 the Intercollegiate Socialist Society with chapters on many campuses. In 1921, the Society changed its name to the League for Industrial Democracy (L.I.D.) and set up the Student L.I.D.

The Marxists extended their socialist influence at our universities during the Great Depression of the 1930's, and broadened that influence as a result of the heavy influx into our institutions of German and Austrian socialist and Communist refugees from Hitlerism.

During the sincere and patriotic but sometimes ill-informed, careless and tactless campaign against communism led by U.S. Senator Joseph R. McCarthy in the 1950's, the Marxists successfully used the charge of "McCarthyism" as a shield to protect themselves from any investigation or criticism of their subversive teaching, and they still continue to do so, though Senator McCarthy died in 1957.

In 1962, the Student League for Industrial Democracy changed its name to Students for a Democratic Society. At that time there were only 4,000 American military advisers in Vietnam and President John F. Kennedy had not yet sent there thousands of our GI's.

In 1964, Students for a Democratic Society and other revolutionary communist youth groups, along with Marxist faculty members, instigated the campus demonstrations and riots at the University of California at Berkeley. In that year, too, Marxist faculty members emerged as leaders of "teach-ins" on and off campus against the Vietnam War, after the American people had become involved in a second "no-win" or "limited" war against a Communist enemy in Asia. The

first such war against a Communist enemy was fought under
the aegis of the United Nations by Americans in Korea. In
that war, as now in Vietnam, the power of Socialist propaganda prevented an American victory by inducing the United
States to refrain from using its full military and spiritual
strength.

Had the Vietnam War been fought against a non-Communist enemy, it is probable that the campus "teach-ins" at our
universities would not have taken place. Marxists are not, as
they claim, for "peace," that is, for indivisible peace for
everybody under all circumstances. Marxists are for peace se-
lectively. They are not against all wars; on the contrary, they
are *for* all wars that extend communism and are *against* wars
that weaken it. They describe as morally "just" all wars for
communism and wars against advanced capitalism ("wars of
liberation against imperialism," or "wars against colonialism"—as they put it). Marxists are not in favor, of course,
of wars against Soviet or Red Chinese imperialism and colonialism, such as in Tibet, 1951, in Hungary, 1956, and in the
ruthless suppression of Czechoslovakia, 1968. Marxists claim
sole moral right to distinguish between "just" and "unjust"
wars, and are unwilling to fight for any kind of freedom
except Socialist "freedom" under a Marxian dictatorship.

In 1939, for example, when the Soviet Union attacked
little Finland, many Marxists in the United States sent tele-
grams to President Franklin D. Roosevelt urging him to ask
Congress to declare war on Finland. In 1940, when the
Hitler-Stalin Pact was in force, radical Marxists in our country were bitterly opposed to any American military intervention in the Allied war against Hitler. It was only when he rup-
tured his pact with Stalin, and Nazi Germany suddenly
attacked the Soviet Union, "first land of socialism," in June
1941, that American radicals of the Left began to clamor for
U.S. military opposition to Hitler.

In our country today, the Vietnam War—branded as an
"unjust" war by Marxists because it is being fought against a
Communist power—is a tool used for advocacy of "resistance
culture" against all phases of capitalist enterprise and traditional culture. The radical Leftists are aware that opposition

to the Vietnam War is a mighty but merely temporarily useful tool. It will have to be replaced by some other tool for stirring up people's emotions whenever an uneasy peace based on a cease-fire is achieved in Vietnam.

THE REAL CREDIBILITY GAP

To try to help preserve our Western civilization from degradation by "resistance culture," I have been reporting on Socialist activities in our nation for the last twenty years. In 1965, keenly aware of growing Socialist subversion on our campuses and in our communities, I resolved that whenever possible I would attend meetings held by the revolutionary communist Students for a Democratic Society, by the radical "New Politics" groups, and by the Socialist Scholars Conference, radical Marxist academic membership group.

Until the SDS rebellion at Columbia University broke out in April 1968, very few academicians and university administrators heeded the warnings in my reports. Among them, to the best of my knowledge, only Chancellor Maurice B. Mitchell of the University of Denver read and believed my piece "Ten Days in April," and early in March 1968 he made effective plans to cope with any violent illegal faculty and student activity on his campus.

For his attention, I am very grateful. Still more, I am grateful to Robert M. Bleiberg, courageous and farsighted editor of *Barron's*, who published my articles about the revolutionary Leftist radicals and made my reporting available not only to that publication's subscribers but also, on newsstands across the nation, to the general public.

After *Barron's* published "Ten Days in April" about the subversive SDS meeting in Weinstein Hall at New York University, the campus newspaper *Washington Square Journal* carried an editorial, March 21, 1968, that was headed "RED BAITING (AGAIN) and stated: "Columnist Alice Widener has seen fit to shine her benevolent enlightening truth on the state of the New Left. She takes as case in point the recent weekend conference of regional SDS in Weinstein subcellar.

Mrs. Widener said she not only senses a new Bolshevik Revolution, but, among other things, she said the conference gave her the impression that University officials do not know what is brewing under them (they probably do) . . . Mrs. Widener has spread what at the very least must be called misinformation on the front page of the business paper *Barron's* . . . Until the Village Independent Democrats turn into another Petrograd Societ, there's little cause to worry about revolution. Weinstein subcellar will hold dances and Mrs. Widener will be yelling in a corner somewhere about something."

Perhaps I should have yelled instead of written about the SDS regional meeting at New York University. I should have yelled loud enough to rouse the trustees and administrators from their dream-world sleep. Or I should have done something eccentric enough to attract newsworthy attention from NBC, CBS and ABC and gained a nationwide forum on a newscast or talk-show to warn Americans in February 1968 about the young radicals' revolutionary plans and activities. In 1969 and 1970, their faces appeared on newspaper front pages and TV screens throughout the world as perpetrators of violence that cost innocent lives and destroyed valuable property, including irreplaceable research documents.

One of the persons mentioned in my "Red baiting" article about the SDS regional meeting at N.Y.U. was Bernardine Dohrn, an SDS leader now a fugitive from U.S. justice. Miss Dohrn is on the F.B.I.'s "most wanted" list and was indicted by a grand jury in Detroit for her alleged role in bombings designed to kill people.

The alleged "misinformation" in my article "Ten Days in April" on *Barron's* front page, March 11, 1968, is now recognized by government authorities as solid information attested to, for example, by Bernardine Dohrn in her own handwriting. On October 30, 1970, the Senate Internal Security Subcommittee released a photographic reproduction of her diary. She left it in her apartment when she fled from justice and it is now in the hands of the Chicago police. An entry in the diary for Saturday, February 10, 1968, is marked in her own handwriting "SDS regional."

Miss Dohrn was there in Weinstein subcellar. She and the

Smiling soon after their arrival at Kennedy International Airport, N.Y. on 1/9/66 from a self-appointed peace mission are, L-R: leftist student organizer Thomas Hayden, Yale Univ. history professor, Staughton Lynd, and New York City Communist theoretician, Herbert Aptheker. Reporting on their trip, Lynd stated that North Vietnamese Premier Pham Van Dong had denied that regular troops from his country are fighting in South Vietnam.   UPI others present said and did exactly what I wrote that they said and did. The only "misinformation" given to the public about the meeting at New York University was by Chancellor Allan Cartter and Vice Chancellor Harold Whiteman and by the editors of the campus newspaper, the *Washington Square Journal*. Had they acted as objective fact-finders instead of defensive apologists, and had they discharged their civic and social responsibility by publicly denouncing the SDS leaders of the subversive meeting, there undoubtedly would have been a lot less bloodshed, physical injuries and destruction of property on campuses throughout our nation.

Today, all federal and state criminal investigative agencies in our country recognize that the SDS regional meeting in Weinstein Hall subcellar in February 1968 was an event of major significance in the American radical Leftist revolutionary movement.

Robert M. Bleiberg, editor of *Barron's*, and I tried hard to forestall violence in our country on and off campus by issuing factual reports on what the militant radicals were writing, saying and doing.

Unhappily, it was the Marxist teachers of destruction and their pupils who prevailed.

It is not too late to rescue our freedom, I hope with all my heart.

In 1976, our nation will celebrate its two-hundredth anniversary. Will it be celebrated as Radical America, according to the Socialist Scholars' and fellow Marxists' desire, or as Soviet America, according to the Communist International's desire, or will our nation celebrate the anniversary as our beloved United States of America, according to the American majority's desire?

The answer to that question will be determined, I believe, by the quality of judgment exercised by the American people in the matter of national priorities, which are a principal matter of current discussion by "The Movement." As in all their discussions, the Old and New Leftists, all Marxists of one kind or another, pay keenest destructive attention to the first four priorities set forth in the Preamble of our Constitution, a document written by the Founding Fathers of our nation, men who put first things first. They knew, as do contemporary Marxists, that on the first four priorities hang all the rest of our general welfare and liberty. If the radicals can destroy the first four, they can destroy the subsequent ones.

As set forth in the Preamble, the aims of our Constitution are, in order of priority: First, "to form a more perfect union;" second, "to establish justice;" third, "to insure domestic tranquility;" and fourth, "to provide for the common defense."

The Marxist teachers of destruction seek to destroy our union as a people through fomenting every kind of dissension by means of "class struggle." They seek to destroy our justice, mainly based on Anglo-Saxon common law, through wrecking the dignified impartiality of our courts and setting up the kind of "people's justice" that exists in the Socialist nations wherein The State is judge, jury, prosecutor and sole defense attorney. They seek to destroy our domestic tranquility by aggravating discontent, envy, and all natural, genuine or fancied ills in our fallible human society, and by instigating riots and demonstrations certain to lead to violence. They seek to destroy our common military defense by undermining the morale and might of our armed forces, and by wrecking the productive capacity of our great industries, which make weapons for our defense and consumer goods for our prosperity and well-being.

If we permit the Socialist Scholars and their like to persuade us to neglect our real priorities, we shall lose the blessings of liberty.

If we put first things first—as does the Preamble of our Constitution—we shall form a more perfect union through enlightened realism, better understanding and greater compassion; we shall establish justice that is swift, sure and impartial; we shall insure domestic tranquility by enforcing proper regard for law and order; and we shall provide what is necessary for the common military defense.

Then, having attended to the first four priorities, we shall possibly be able to triumph over adversity, promote the general welfare, and secure the blessings of liberty for ourselves and our posterity.

Chapter 1

LONG PREPARATION
FOR REVOLUTION

IN THE AFTERMATH of the student revolt at the University of California in Berkeley, 1964, a shocked and bewildered American public asked about the youthful rioters, "Where did they come from? What kind of background have they?"

Later, in the spring of 1965, after several thousand young people had taken part in an Easter march on Washington, D.C., April 17, to protest against United States policy in Vietnam, and later still in August, when dozens of students accompanied by some Ivy League professors defied the law in the District of Columbia, penetrated the White House to stage a sit-in, and attempted to break through police barricades at the Capitol, the stunned general public again asked about the demonstrators and practitioners of civil disobedience, "Where did they come from?"

This same question was on the lips of onlookers in New York City and other communities as there took place so-called "peace" parades and demonstrations, October 15 and 16, 1965, led by notorious Leftists who were followed by thousands of young people, many unkempt, among whom some carried poles with dangling puppet-effigies of a devilish Uncle Sam dripping with blood, and of a sadistic President of the United States, dressed in black and carrying a banner inscribed, "Kill, kill, kill!"

As I stood on a street corner, observing the astonished faces of bystanders whose Saturday afternoon stroll along Fifth Avenue was so rudely interrupted, and watching the aggressive young Leftists parade, two lines of a poem learned in childhood flashed sardonically through my mind—"Where did you come from, baby dear? Out of the nowhere into the here?"

SDS OFFSPRING OF SOCIALIST LEAGUE

Trying to recall the poem, I was aware of the origin of a group in the forefront of youthful Leftist activities in our country, Students for a Democratic Society. It is the legitimate offspring of the socialist League for Industrial Democracy, 112 East 19th St., New York City.

For sixty-five years, the League has been training up young Americans in the Leftist way they should not go.

Several shelves in my library are stacked with League for Industrial Democracy official publications, dating from 1911, six years after the Leftist group was first organized as the Intercollegiate Socialist Society (ISS).

The term "industrial democracy" is to be found in the April-May 1919 issue of the ISS publication in an article by the late Alexander Trachtenberg, then a member of the Yale University chapter of the ISS and later, head of the Communist publishing house "International Publishers" in New York City.

In 1919, Alexander Trachtenberg wrote for the ISS (later, L.I.D.):

"The Russian revolution is the heritage of the world. It must not be defeated by foreign militarism. It must live, so that Russia may be truly free and, through its freedom, blaze the way for industrial democracy throughout the world."

(In England, Beatrice and Sidney Webb, enthusiastic admirers of the Bolshevik Revolution in Russia, had adopted the term "industrial democracy" to describe the kind of socialist government they wished their Fabian Society to foist on the British people.)

SUB ROSA AT FIRST

In 1945, Dr. Harry A. Overstreet, long-time friend of the League for Industrial Democracy, said at its 40th anniversary, Hotel Roosevelt, February 3, New York City:

". . . I can remember the time when this organization was just starting meeting with a number of teachers of the University of California, very apprehensively and timidly making an effort to study this terrible thing called socialism.

"We studied socialism and we didn't want anybody to know we were doing it. And out here your League started the process of getting college people to think about the things that need to be thought of. . . ."

For decades in our country, the League for Industrial Democracy exerted tutelage over its progeny in the Student League for Industrial Democracy (S.L.I.D.), educating them into thinking about the things which socialists deemed necessary to be thought of—such as government ownership of the means of production and Marxist "production for use and not for profit"—and subsidizing students' activities as they installed a kind of *sub rosa* socialist "light" on the American college campus. Today that light is not only out in the open, its flaming red rays are sweeping across the nation.

The April 3, 1965 L.I.D. pamphlet "60 Years of Democratic Education" contains a brief history of the League for Industrial Democracy by its executive director emeritus, Harry W. Laidler, who wrote that after World War II:

". . . the League began again to organize college chapters under the able and dedicated direction of Jesse Cavileer, James Farmer [now Assistant Secretary for Administration in the U. S. Department of Health, Education and Welfare (HEW)] and others.

"In 1962 the Executive Committee of the S.L.I.D. voted to change the name of the League's student affiliate to the Students for a Democratic Society. The SDS is now the largest intercollegiate society on the American campus and, under the secretaryship of C. Clark Kissinger, is doing yeoman service in the field of civil rights, peace, academic freedom and community organization among the poor. . . .

"The general society since World War II has continued with vigor and effectiveness. . . . Tom Kahn, author of *The Economics of Equality* is now the League's able executive . . . Michael Harrington, author of *The Other America,* to whom great credit is due for his outstanding work in pressing for the present war on poverty, was elected Chairman of the Board. . . ."

SOCIALIST LEAGUE TAX-EXEMPT

As an "educational" organization, the League for Industrial Democracy has long enjoyed tax-exempt status granted by the Internal Revenue Service, and has used part of L.I.D. funds to subsidize the student offspring organization Students for a Democratic Society. But in 1965 the SDS' activist role in a Liberal-radical coalition jeopardized the L.I.D.'s tax-exemption.

On October 4, the L.I.D. and Paul Booth, national secretary of SDS, announced "for tax reasons" the amicable severance of SDS from the parent L.I.D.

The severance seemed to be mostly for material reasons. It isn't logical to assume otherwise, for the L.I.D. was well aware of what its "children" were doing. The L.I.D. pamphlet "To Build a New World" by Thomas R. Brooks, published in 1965, contained the following printed statement:

"Students for a Democratic Society is the student department of the L.I.D. It seeks to bring together all those—liberals and radicals, activists and scholars—who share its vision of a truly democratic society. Among the most active groups on the campus scene, the SDS strives to implement its vision and analysis by engaging students in study-action projects, both through its campus chapter structure and through the community organizing projects administered by SDS's Economic Research and Action Project."

APING RUSSIAN STRATEGY

Concerning Students for a Democratic Society, offspring of the socialist L.I.D. in which he is chairman, Michael Harrington wrote in a column datelined February 21, 1965, Ann Arbor, Michigan:

"I talked to some American Narodniks at the University of Michigan last week.

"The original Narodniks were Russian students who, in the summer of 1874, went out to preach a mystical populism to the peasants. Whenever someone asked where they were going they said, 'To the Narod' [meaning] to the people. The adventure did not last long. The police cracked down. . . .

"The young students at Ann Arbor with whom I spoke were activists of the Economic Research and Action Project (ERAP) at Ann Arbor, sponsored by the Students for a Democratic Society. They have already accomplished more than their Russian forerunners. But they and an increasingly larger number of students on the campus have embraced the Narodnik principle: To the people."

Mr. Harrington explained that members of ERAP work in the slums, in the South on civil rights situations, and among "the American poor." He predicted for ERAP in the 1960's an organizing power in the big city poor, black and white, similar to CIO organizing power among factory workers in the 1930's. Then L.I.D. chairman Harrington summed up, "the New Narodniks represent a first class event. . . . In the near political future the voices of these experienced idealists will be heard."

There is no doubt that SDS is practicing the Russian revolutionary Narodnik strategy, as Michael Harrington openly boasts.

BEAT-THE-DRAFT ACTIVITIES

The result is so damaging to our nation that on October 24, 1965, the *New York Daily News* reported:

". . . Attorney General Nicholas Katzenbach disclosed that the Justice Department is probing the anti-draft movement. Speaking in Chicago, headquarters of Students for a Democratic Society, Katzenbach said 'some Communists' were mixed up in the pacifist program.

"Katzenbach said the Students for a Democratic Society was but one of many New Left groups being investigated. . . .

"Also under scrutiny was a mimeographed pamphlet circulated in California. . . 'Brief Notes on the Ways and Means of Beating and Defeating the Draft' . . ."

The mimeographed pamphlet referred to by *The News* counsels registrants to pose as conscientious objectors, to feign homosexuality, show up for draft examinations either drunk or "high" on narcotics, and bribe a doctor for a disability certificate.

The *New York Daily News* continued its October 24 report:

"The Students for a Democratic Society disavowed, through Paul Booth, national secretary, any connection with this draft-dodger's guide. But Booth announced that the society [SDS] was expanding to enlist even high school students. In addition to encouraging youths to file as conscientious objectors, he said, SDS members are to picket draft board offices, distribute pacifist tracts, attack local draft boards as 'undemocratic' and recruiters and officer trainees as 'war criminals' ".

On October 25, the *New York Journal-American* reported on the "Beat the Draft" movement's activities in the city high schools, and quoted from a newsletter distributed by the Committee to End the War in Vietnam stating:

"We are excited about the proposal offered by Todd Gitlin of SDS on the setting up of information centers for confused draftees and young men about to be drafted, informing them of all the alternatives to fighting in Vietnam—moral, legal and technical—open to them."

The newsletter went on to state, "We are planning an intensive anti-induction campaign on city college campuses next year. . . ."

Who is Todd Gitlin and where did he come from?

Almost no one in the press or general public ever has heard his name. But the League for Industrial Democracy knows very well who he is, for its 60th anniversary commemorative pamphlet, April 3, 1965, lists "Todd Gitlin" as a member of the L.I.D. board of directors.

Though the big press is now full of feature stories and think pieces about SDS, it is the little Leftist press that tells the inside stories and provides the most pertinent facts and information. For example, an article by Steven Kelman (then a Long Island student, now a Harvard graduate, class of 1970, and author of "Push Comes to Shove") in the September 27 issue of the socialist magazine *The New Leader*, began with the following statement:

"In the fall of 1964 identical letters appeared in a number of liberal and radical magazines. The missives were signed by the aged pacifist A. J. Muste, radical journalist I. F. Stone, and W. H. Ferry of the Center for the Study of Democratic Institutions. 'We want to inform your readers,' they said, 'about a critical new development on the American political scene—the emergence of an organization of students and young people who are seriously committed to building a new American left.'

"The organization was the Students for a Democratic Society (SDS). . . .

"Officially, SDS is the student wing of the League for Industrial Democracy. . . .

"In 1960, the League . . . decided to revitalize its old moribund student division. . . A new constitution described SDS as 'an association of young people on the left' and extended an invitation to 'liberals and radicals, activists and scholars, students and faculty.' SDS then got off the ground with an 'inspirational founding convention' in 1962 at Port Huron, Michigan. . .''

This shows clearly that the League was fully aware of, and even instigated, the SDS association with "radicals" and "activists."

"OLD LEFT" vs "NEW LEFT"

Mr. Kelman went on to explain the difference between the "Old Left" and "New Left" in our country, a difference having little to do with age, though the adult sponsors of the "New Left" pretend that it is a self-originating movement of "youngsters."

"Tom Kahn of the L.I.D.," reported Steven Kelman in *The New Leader,* "is at 27 considered a member of the 'Old Left,' while octogenarian A.J. Muste is a 'New Left' prophet and hero' ".

The difference between Old and New Left was thus explained by Steven Kelman: The Old Left wants Bayard

Rustin's proposal, which is supported by the L.I.D., for a coalition of Negro and labor groups with the left wing of the Democratic Party in order to bring about what Rustin calls "revolutionary social change." But—according to Kelman—the SDS and Rustin-L.I.D. proposals are very different, so different that former Yale Assistant Professor Staughton Lynd, "who has become a sort of faculty sponsor for the New Left," denounced Rustin's proposal. What Students for a Democratic Society wants to accomplish—reported Steven Kelman—is creation of *"an independent national organization of the poor."*

SDS calls this kind of social-political organization "participatory democracy." Steven Kelman explained in *The New Leader:* "Even now, SDS' own internal participatory democracy is producing proposals for elitist social action. Staughton Lynd has proposed that activists against the war in Vietnam set up *an alternative government* which would collect taxes from people who refused to pay their taxes to the Federal government, and conduct 'war crimes trials' against President Johnson and Secretary [of Defense] McNamara. . . ."

Another view of the L.I.D.'s offspring, Students for a Democratic Society, is presented in the September-October 1965 issue of the pro-Communist publication *Young Socialist.* On page 22, it reports: "STUDENT TO SPEAK ON VIETNAM TRIP: Carl Oglesby, president of SDS, will be touring college campuses this fall, speaking against the Vietnam war. During his visit to South Vietnam this summer, he was able to talk with members of the [Communist] National Liberation Front, and will be able to give a first-hand account of what is taking place."

It is interesting to note the description of SDS president Carl Oglesby as a "student" in *Young Socialist.* He is otherwise described as "30, drop-out, playwright, technical writer" in a caption under his photograph in *The New York Times Magazine,* November 7, 1965, which carried a most sympathetic lead article on the SDS by Thomas R. Brooks, a member of the executive committee of the League for Industrial Democracy, parent of SDS.

The editor of *Young Socialist,* Doug Jenness, described the present day internecine socialist struggle in our country, a dispute which does not differ at all from the old Bolshevik-Menshevik struggle in Russia, and which is as alien to the basic design of Americanism as the Kremlin is architecturally alien to the White House. Mr. Jenness wrote:

"The conflict that has been raging in the peace movement since the SDS March on Washington is a *political conflict* between those like [Bayard] Rustin, [Norman] Thomas, and [David] McReynolds* who still want to maintain a coalition with the Democratic Party and the New Radicals who see the Democratic Party, the 'liberal wing' notwithstanding, as the enemy and want to organize an opposition to it. . . .

"The New Radicals who see the need for a social revolution in this country must be extremely clear about the pitfalls of reformist and coalition politics and must formulate for themselves a consistent revolutionary perspective. The logic of breaking with the Democratic Party and its Socialist servants like Rustin is to create an independent political organization that aspires to lead and organize a social revolution.

"However, to realize the necessity of changing this rotten society from top to bottom, in order to put an end to the kind of wars the U. S. is waging in Viet Nam does not cut across the very important job of organizing as large a protest as possible around the specific issue of getting American troops out of Viet Nam. . . ."

The foregoing, as anyone familiar with Communist doctrine can see, is standard Red operating procedure for forming a "temporary alliance" with non-Communist forces to gain a specific objective while at the same time maintaining the separate Communist political identity for revolutionary leadership.

On page 22 of the September-October 1965 issue of the pro-Communist *Young Socialist* magazine, there is a note praising SDS for adopting "anti Red-baiting amendments" to its constitution and thus establishing SDS as "an open

---

*On November 6, 1965, David McReynolds publicly burned his draft card.

non-exclusive organization willing to work with all those who have agreement on certain basic issues."

Toward the end of World War II, in February 1945, Upton Sinclair, who founded the L.I.D. in 1905, addressed the League's 40th anniversary symposium on "The Task Ahead," and said: "Production for use and not for profit—you, friends of the League for Industrial Democracy, are not frightened when you hear that slogan. The private owners of industry are frightened, but that is because they do not understand what is happening, and cannot see the world can get along without private owners of industry."

Today in America it is not only the private owners of industry who are frightened and shocked at what the Left is doing in our country. The United States Government itself and the vast majority of Americans are shocked at the activities of young Leftists.

SUBSIDIZED REVOLUTIONARIES

And yet, what Upton Sinclair said in 1945 is true in 1970, for it seems that the leaders of American industry and the innocent bystanders who watch young and old socialists demonstrating against U. S. foreign policy and disobeying the laws of our country still "do not understand what is happening."

L.I.D. executive committee member Thomas R. Brooks quoted in his *New York Times* article of November 7, 1965 the statement by SDS president Carl Oglesby that the student organization had been receiving money from "richies" and from "friendly institutions."

It still does.

Congress should find out who are the rich individuals and friendly institutions helping to subsidize the Students for a Democratic Society in their attempts to create a social revolution through their Economic Research and Action Project among "the poor," and their illegal marches and campus revolts.

Where do the SDS leaders get the money to be so mobile, traveling from one end of our country to another, paying for the expensive communications—postage, long distance phone calls, airplane and train tickets, printed publications and leaflets?

Certainly the hardworking taxpayers who are paying for our war effort in Vietnam have a right to know who is subsidizing homegrown Leftist support of the enemy.

Just as obviously, however, the facts about where the SDS itself comes from are evident, for it is a matter of public record.

Students for a Democratic Society—the "youth" organization working for creation of an independent political organization for social revolution in our nation—comes directly from the socialist League for Industrial Democracy which set out deliberately, 65 years ago, to abolish capitalism in the United States and convert our country into a Socialist State by means of "promoting an intelligent interest in socialism among college men and women."

On the 40th anniversary of the L.I.D. in 1945, Harry Laidler, then its executive director, said the organization was anxious, as soon as circumstances permitted, "to develop again its college work with renewed vigor" and "to stir" the youth intellectually.

In Students for a Democratic Society the American people now have a chance to take a good look at the youth which the L.I.D. has stirred with its socialist "college work."

By their fruits ye shall know them.

It is dangerously naive for any innocent American spectator of SDS activism to believe it is a spontaneous youthful rebellion coming out of the nowhere into the here. It is equally dangerous for patriotic American adults to dismiss the voting-age "Narodniks" as idealistic, prankish "youngsters."

Where do they come from?

The answer to this question is that they come from well-subsidized, mostly tax-exempt, long-established homegrown socialist organizations, where they are carefully trained by highly experienced leaders growing bolder and bolder as a result of their success in capturing extremely influential positions in our universities, churches, labor unions, communications media, and even in the executive, legislative and judicial branches of our Federal government.

Chapter 2

SOCIALIST SCHOLARS
SHOW THEIR HAND

EARLY IN THE morning of September 11, 1965, I took pencil and paper, boarded a bus, and rode uptown to McMillin Theater at Columbia University, New York City, to attend the first panel of the First Annual Conference of Socialist Scholars.

Originally, the conference had been scheduled to take place at Rutgers University in New Jersey. But—explained Professor Louis Menashe of Polytechnic Institute, Brooklyn, N. Y., an organizer of the conference—owing to the present "intolerant" climate at Rutgers, the conference was transferred to Columbia.

The "intolerant climate" at Rutgers was caused by State Senator Wayne Dumont Jr., who had called for the removal from the Rutgers faculty of Professor Eugene D. Genovese because of his remarks at the Rutgers teach-in on Vietnam, in April: "Those of you who know me know I am a Marxist and a Socialist. Therefore, unlike most of my distinguished colleagues here this morning, I do not fear or regret the impending Viet Cong victory in Vietnam. I welcome it."

Governor Richard J. Hughes of New Jersey declared on August 6, 1965, that "however offensive" the professor's statement might be to individual members of the board of trustees of Rutgers, it did not constitute grounds for dismissal. A few days later, State Senator Dumont, undaunted, again called for dismissal of Prof. Genovese and appeared on NBC-TV in a discussion of the controversial case.

This evidently led the sponsors of the First Annual Conference of Socialist Scholars to shift their assembly away from Rutgers to Columbia University.

Though hospitable, the climate at Columbia's McMillin Theater on Saturday morning was most uncomfortable. The weather was hot and humid; there was no air-conditioning; the theater doors were kept shut.

Panel One began at 9:30 and there were several hundred people in the attentive audience of adults and students.

The chairman was Professor H. H. Wilson of Princeton University. The topic was "Class and Ideology." Richard Hamilton of Princeton, an associate professor of sociology, presented a paper "Working Class Authoritarianism: A Reconsideration." Prof. Eleanor B. Leacock, anthropologist of Polytechnic Institute in Brooklyn, presented a paper "Distortions of Working Class Reality in American Social Sciences." Panel commentators on these papers were Prof. Vernon K. Dibble of Columbia University and Prof. James F. Becker of New York University.

DOUBLE-TALK

In the presentation of papers and during the commentaries on them, it became evident that by "authoritarian" the speakers meant "anti-Communist, anti-Marxist, anti-radical-Socialist," and by "tolerant" they meant tolerant of, or sympathetic to, radicalism, Marxism, socialism and communism.

The most intolerant sectors of the American population, Prof. Hamilton found, are "the farmers, the self-employed middle class, and the factory foremen. "

Another group under attack by the panel for "authoritarianism" (defined as intolerance of "dissident political minorities such as the Communist Party"), were the veterans' organizations which were described as being "under elite regimes."

Professor Leacock of Polytechnic Institute in Brooklyn, a thin, intense and very articulate woman, sharply attacked the middle-class education aim of guiding children and students toward the goals of "striving and taking individual responsibility." Prof. Leacock found that in the United States "a truly dying system is in such desperate need for a revolutionary system to dig its grave."

What she decries in the present school system is emphasis "on orderliness and the narrowest interpretation of patriotism which makes it virtually impossible for them [the teachers] to teach."

To correct this, Prof. Leacock suggests a "change of materials" in the schools, and also a search to determine "what are the sources for unified, militant action."

Vernon K. Dibble of Columbia University, a fat little man with a big mustache, said that what is necessary in consideration of class ideology is "structural fragmentation conducive to tolerance." He used a great deal of academic jargon to put across his point that the existing system of American society must be broken up in order to bring it under the control of radicals.

Prof. James F. Becker of New York University said it is necessary "to develop programs for the dissident minorities to modify the existing structure of social power. It is necessary to give them the levers they need." He paused and then, despite his professed disapproval of emotional rhetorical appeal, burst out, indeed almost shouted out, "When the time is ripe to make demands, *much* must be demanded!"

In the reverberations of applause, I silently reminded myself of Samuel Johnson's teaching that human beings must have fortitude of mind and body. It was so hot in the auditorium that I was miserable.

On the other side of the hall, an indignant young man, wanting to make sure, I suppose, that he was keeping the right Left company, demanded to know what Professor Hamilton of Princeton meant by "tolerance."

The Professor rushed to the microphone.

"All the remarks I made," he said cuttingly, "have to do with *a specific kind* of tolerance."

His reply almost brought down the house. With a burst of enthusiastic applause, the audience showed they knew exactly what he meant.

Professor Eugene D. Genovese, formerly of Rutgers University, New Jersey. He is now at the University of Rochester, New York. In the April 1965 teach-in, at Rutgers he said, "Those of you who know me know I am a Marxist and a Socialist..." At the First Socialist Scholars Conference at Columbia University, he said, "...The political separation—activist and academician—is a matter of convenience . . . That we all know." At the Second Socialist Scholars Conference he said, ". . .We ought to be delighted every time a worker steals something from his plant. . ." Here he is addressing a Rutgers University students teach-in, April 19, 1966.   UPI

I laughed, sardonically. As if it were yesterday, I could hear bewildered, shocked President Harry Truman tell reporters, on his return from the Potsdam Conference in 1945, "The Communists don't mean the same thing by the word 'democracy' that we do."

After two or three more questions from the floor, Prof. H. H. Wilson of Princeton announced the end of the session, and said Panel Two would take place after lunch.

As I left the theater, a good looking young man in his early thirties and a young clergyman in clerical garb with a big cross dangling from a heavy chain on his chest were ahead of me. "Well, you know," said the clergyman, "I'm an anarchist."

Lunch over, I went back to McMillin Theater to attend Panel Two of the First Annual Conference of Socialist Scholars.

The chairman was Paul M. Sweezy, editor of the radical Leftist *Monthly Review*. The topic was "Contemporary Forms of Imperialism." The speaker was Conor Cruise O'Brien, then occupying a chair of humanities at New York University, previously a member of the Irish delegation to the United Nations, and U. N. envoy to Katanga in the Congo during 1961 at the height of the troubles there.

VIRULENT ANTI-AMERICANISM

On June 20, 1965, Irving Kristol wrote a review for the *New York Herald Tribune* of Conor Cruise O'Brien's book of essays *Writers and Politics*. It appeared under the *Trib* caption "A Back of the Hand to Uncle Sam." Mr. Kristol wrote:

"The essays and tid-bits in *Writers and Politics* [O'Brien's book] . . . are very much the work of an ideological guerrilla. If any single theme can be said to unite them, it is virulent anti-Americanism; the United States is the new Ascendancy, its intellectuals are hypocritical priests of capitalism, its masses are bigoted and servile, and for the free, progressive spirit it [the United States] is The Enemy incarnate. . . . "

After O'Brien had temporarily ceased waging ideological guerrilla warfare against the United States (only because panel time was growing short), Professor A. Norman Klein of Bennington College entered the fray. "The United States," he declared scathingly, "has become the world center for export of counter-revolution." Then he exhausted all the tired old Socialist clichés about "The Pentagon" as a symbol of all that is evil, without once referring to or denouncing any Red Army institution.

Professor Said Shah, from India, a professor at State University of New York at Plattsburg, was the next speaker. His first scholarly comments were about himself.

"When they heard about my coming here, they threatened at the University in Plattsburg that they would fire me," he said. He threw back his head and grinned widely at the audience. "You see," he hissed derisively into the microphone, "I'm here!"

The audience roared with laughter, cheered and applauded.

As Prof. Said Shah began to attack American foreign policy in a very British-accented voice, I quietly rose and left the theater.

I cannot comment, therefore, on what panelist Prof. Timothy Harding of California State College at Los Angeles said about Conor Cruise O'Brien's paper on imperialism. A heavy-set man with a heavy beard, Prof. Harding nodded several times as O'Brien made his meanest anti-Americanisms, so I take it that Prof. Harding was mostly in agreement. His demeanor—to borrow Prof. Hamilton's descriptive term—was very "tolerant."

Tired on Sunday morning, I skipped Panel Three of the Conference. The topic was "American Conservatism." The chairman was Alan Trachtenberg of Pennsylvania State University; the speakers were Allen Guttmann of Amherst College and Warren I. Susman of Rutgers University. The commentators were Aileen S. Kraditor of Rhode Island College and Norman Dain of Rutgers.

Resting at home, I studied the publication *Studies on the Left*. Several of the editors—Eugene D. Genovese, Staughton Lynd and Norman Fruchter—were participants in the Socialist Scholars Conference. So was associate editor Warren Susman.

The editorial tenor of *Studies on the Left* can be determined by the following comment on page 3 of the Spring 1965 issue:

"FROM THE EDITORS:
   "In the past *Studies* has concentrated on the broad contours of American social structure and history; now it focuses on specific problems of social revolution in this country. This makes the magazine identify with 'insurgent forces'; people in the civil rights movement, community unions, trade unions, student organizations, radical intellectuals and artists. . . ."

The Sunday luncheon of the Socialist Scholars Conference was held in the dining room of John Jay Hall at Columbia University. Afterwards there took place a business meeting presided over by Professor Helmut Gruber of Polytechnic Institute, Brooklyn. He was a main organizer of the conference, and it was partly subsidized by the Louis M. Rabinowitz Foundation, Inc., of 30 East 42nd Street, New York, N.Y. 10017. (The present president of the foundation is Victor Rabinowitz; Lucille Perlman is vice-president, and Marsha G. Rabinowitz is secretary-treasurer. The foundation was incorporated in 1944. In 1967, the Rabinowitz Foundation subsidized *Where It's At*, by Jill Hamberg, Paul Booth, Mimi Feingold and Carl Wittman, a research guide for revolutionary community organizing widely distributed by Students for a Democratic Society, the National Council of Churches' Department of Social Justice, the Radical Education Project and other radical groups.)

PROFESSORS AS REVOLUTIONARIES

At McMillin Theater, when Panel Four began on Sunday afternoon, the weather was cooler but the radicalism was hotter. The topic was "The Future of American Socialism," and it was termed the over-all theme of the conference by chairman Ann J. Lane of Sarah Lawrence College. The panel discussion leader was Professor Staughton Lynd of Yale University who
• has been affiliated with the pro-Peking Progressive Labor Party;

- has been affiliated with the Socialist Workers' Party and American Youth for Democracy, both of which were cited as subversive by a U. S. Attorney General;
- was arrested for trying to break through the police barricades at the Capitol, August 9, 1965;
- called for "civil disobedience so persistent and massive" that the President, Secretary of State, Secretary of Defense and other high U. S. Government officials would have to resign.

The "discussants" on Panel Four were Norman Fruchter, Sylvester Leaks, Herbert Aptheker, and Prof. Eugene D. Genovese.

Wearing a yellow shirt with rolled up sleeves, Prof. Lynd stood at a rostrum with a microphone to address the audience. He began by saying the main question to be answered is, "What is to be done?" A Socialist scholar, he said, should be ready at any moment to put aside his books and devote himself "to the jugular" to bring about a better world. Today, he went on, "guerrilla warfare has become a substitute for the breakdown of capitalism." He said that a better world can be brought about only by "a revolutionary instead of reformist" technique. To exert revolutionary means, Prof. Lynd urged "daring and inventive use of civil disobedience." "All of us here are on the same side of the barricades," he said, and later expressed the opinion, "I regard it as reasonable to expect that the American government will wage war at home." Prof. Lynd then examined the role of the Socialist scholar in the academy and said, "I wonder whether every teacher who calls himself a Socialist doesn't have a duty to become a professional revolutionary."

After Prof. Lynd had finished his speech, Herbert Aptheker went to the rostrum. Just a year earlier, almost to the day, he had been in Moscow attending the funeral of Elizabeth Gurley Flynn of the Communist Party, U.S.A. On September 13, 1964, *The Worker* carried a front page report, datelined Moscow, on the Flynn funeral, and announced, "The pallbearers included Herbert Aptheker, representative of the Communist Party of the United States."

Dr. Aptheker began his remarks with the statement, "Professor Lynd's paper opens up everything, as an excellent paper should." He then praised it as "wholly admirable" for showing:

- "desirability of socialism;"
- "necessity of socialism to prevent war;"
- "continuity of the Left;"
- "[Eugene] Debs' historical Bolshevist partisanship;"
- "need for Left unity;"
- "militancy, confidence and modesty."

Dr. Aptheker criticized Prof. Lynd's paper for failing to state that Karl Marx, in his mature years, changed his ideas about the imminence of the coming collapse of capitalism, and also for not pointing out that Lenin predicted there would be "15, 20, perhaps 50 years of war" before Socialist peace could be established.

Communist educator Aptheker then talked about the economic consequences of the United States' "war" economy, and praised Professor Seymour Melman of Columbia University, militant radical and author of *The Peace Race,* for his writings about its effect on our "depleted society." Dr. Aptheker concluded his analysis of Prof. Lynd's paper with the boast, "Not in 30 years has there been such interest in radicalism as there is today, such a sense of confidence, of mass involvement in the radicalization of the United States."

The audience hung on Aptheker's every word and received his remarks with the kind of deferential applause accorded to a hero statesman.

Chairman Ann J. Lane then stepped up to the microphone to introduce the next speaker, Eugene D. Genovese, as "a formerly but never again obscure professor."

The audience roared with laughter.

Dr. Genovese differed with Prof. Staughton Lynd about the desirability of Socialist teachers leaving the campus to become professional revolutionaries. He said that though "time is on our side," it is necessary for Socialist scholars to have patience and fulfill their role as academic intellectuals.

"Though we have good reason to expect American imperialism will be pushed back, we must exert the moral leadership we are prepared to give young radicals." He continued, "We are part of a worldwide movement and our activist allies will help us."

It would be a mistake for Socialist scholars to quit the campus too soon, explained Dr. Genovese, and then he made a statement which shows how naive or ignorant are the boards of trustees and administrators in some of our state-supported and private institutions of higher learning, and which exposes—more clearly than I ever have heard it said—just how cynical is the Leftist radical approach to academic freedom of speech.

"The political separation—activist and academician—is a matter of convenience," he said slowly and sententiously. *"That, we all know."* (Three years later, Genovese resigned from the Socialist Scholars Conference but kept his ideas. For *Newsweek*, July 6, 1970, he wrote that our country faces "a massive breakdown" and said that its root lies "in the palpable failure" of our capitalist system.)

The next speaker was Norman Fruchter, editor of *Studies on the Left*. His thesis was that "The Movement" will come to fruition eventually in a political organization. He said that in desirable situations, "Us disobedients find we are the majority and there aren't even any police left." He said that "to the extent that we have a guerrilla movement in the United States now—there is a network of communications." He talked about The Movement in the Watts area of Los Angeles and predicted there would be "six or seven more cities kicked off in this way."

Mr. Fruchter explained that "the kind of action that Watts indicates is a certain number of white students will go into the ghettoes and begin to work with the explosive black violence in a predominantly political movement."

He said there were "maybe 200 people in the United States who can go into the ghettoes and build an organization." Disastrous subsequent riots in Newark, New Jersey, proved that he knew what he was talking about.

The fourth discussant on Panel Four of the First Annual Socialist Scholars Conference at Columbia University was

Sylvester Leaks of the Harlem Writers Guild, a tall, slim, clean-shaven and well-dressed Negro in suit jacket and necktie. Mr. Leaks is a former feature writer for *Muhammad Speaks* and author of a biography of Malcolm X.*

"BURN, BABY, BURN"

In a clear, well-modulated voice, Mr. Leaks began, "First of all, I'm not non-violent. My leader was assassinated. I believe that slavery and racism are the *sine qua non* of American society." Mr. Leaks said he believes the black *lumpenproletariat* "should go to war *now.*" He said the slogan they need is "Burn, Baby, Burn!"

Somewhat hesitantly, the audience applauded.

"I believe we've got to tear the system down, *now,*" said Sylvester Leaks. "We've got to stop the murderous, barbarous, American-imposed war in Vietnam."

Mr. Leaks said that what is needed is "a complete dismantling of the old morality." He said the white man wouldn't dismantle it; the black man has to do it. He said the black man always had had to help himself all alone.

"Slavery wasn't ended by white armies from the North," he said. "The Negroes in the South ended their own slavery."

To the Socialist Scholars on the stage and to the Communist "scholar" Aptheker, Mr. Leaks hurled the ultimatum, "You had better come to terms with the revolutionary black man, or else—"

Bitterly, Sylvester Leaks demanded to know what the white man ever had done for or with the black man; scornfully, he dismissed all Aptheker's claims of Communist accomplishments.

Next to the fury and flame of his attack on our American society, the Socialist Scholar's attack seemed like a wispy trail of thinnest smoke.

Witheringly, he attacked Staughton Lynd's call for massive and persistent "civil disobedience" as a milksop action.

---

*In 1967, the Louis M. Rabinowitz Foundation gave $3,000 to Sylvester Leaks.

When he had ended his blazing denunciation, which leaped up in flames from a glacier of icy contempt, there was a hush in the theater.

Half apologetically, half defiantly, Prof. Lynd of Yale University said, "I certainly wouldn't want to persuade anyone that we should exhaust the resources of massive civil disobedience before turning to other means."

Chairman Ann J. Lane went to the microphone and said that time was growing late. Then she called on Herbert Aptheker for remarks.

Slowly, and with deliberate calm, he went to the rostrum. The audience was silent. Others had spoken, but this was *the voice,* and his was the word.

TOWARD RADICALIZATION OF AMERICA

"The problem," he began, " is how do we move toward radicalization of America?"

He then said that as he sees it there are five steps toward accomplishment of this aim.

First, he said, is "the battle against war," and he said it could definitely be stated that there *"is now"* such a thing as a battle against war. Briefly, he mentioned the teach-ins and other "peace" activities.

Second, said Aptheker, must be "the all-out effort to achieve greatest possible unity of the Left."

Third, said Dr. Aptheker, "is the Negro Movement. It is now a Negro-white movement. I wish to emphasize the *decisive* character played by [W.E.B.] DuBois, the greatest Negro of this century." Expatiating on this theme, Herbert Aptheker stressed the cooperation between the Marxian Socialists and Dr. DuBois, and his own long association and cooperation with him and with Elizabeth Gurley Flynn and others.

(There was complete stillness in the audience. Aptheker's meaning was crystal clear. He was reminding Sylvester Leaks that it was the Communist Party of the U.S.A. that had spawned, protected and championed W.E.B. DuBois, a long-time Communist who tried to hide his real political affiliation until, shortly before his death in Accra, Ghana, Africa, 1963, he made a pseudo-dramatic move by publicly joining the Communist Party. It organized in his honor the "W.E.B. DuBois Clubs" on many campuses in our country. Aptheker said it was the Communist Party which deserved credit for the "Negro-white" *revolutionary* movement in the United States. And as Aptheker went on developing this subject, there were murmurings of approval and muffled cries of "Yes, yes!" in the audience.)

Fourth, said Aptheker, it was necessary to remember historically that each of the dedicated Marxist radicals who created the revolutionary situation had been "a Deacon for life." He said that the Deacons in the South had learned their role from these dedicated individuals.

Fifth, said Herbert Aptheker, the matter of violence "is not a question for revolutionists. They are not terrorists. Revolutionists, to be effective, cannot be pacifists. The Deacons are not new; they have nothing to do with advocacy of violence; they have to do with resistance, with carrying out the Declaration of Independence."

There was some panel discussion by the various members. Sylvester Leaks said sternly, "I don't think the Deacons should be discussed in public."

They couldn't be so discussed because of their being a gun-toting, outlaw group.

During further exchange of views on several subjects, there was mention of the World War II Warsaw ghetto rebellion and Aptheker linked it historically with the antecedent Nat Turner slave rebellion in the American past.

Then the Communist Party's leading intellectual at the American Institute for Marxist Studies, Dr. Herbert Aptheker, paused dramatically at the rostrum. For a moment he looked at the audience in McMillin Theater. Then he turned deliberately toward Sylvester Leaks.

"Of course," said Communist Aptheker, raising his voice and letting it ring out. "Watts was *glorious*!"

Chapter 3

REVOLUTIONARY
RADICAL COALITION

A NEW LEFTIST revolutionary political force will make it-self felt in our nation during forthcoming elections. The new force will be insidious, disruptive, cunning and confusing; it will back some Republican and some Democratic candidates; it will run its own allegedly "independent" ones on a "new politics" platform in some areas. There will be Communists in the new political revolutionary force; there will be Marxists and socialists. Though widely presented as a "youth" and "peace" movement, the new force has been propelled and led by old-time radicals.

On August 7, 1966, the *Houston Post* carried an article "New Political Force Rising Across U.S." by Paul White. He reported from New York City:

"While Democrats and Republicans worry over Vietnam and party unity, a vast number of leftwing activists, civil rights militants, peace insurgents and Stevenson liberals have established a united front aimed at the Washington administration and altering 'the American way of life.'

"Establishment of the National Conference for New Politics (NCNP) with headquarters in New York comes simultaneously with evidence of its significant success in backing candidates who hold to the 'Morse-Fulbright-Kennedy position' on foreign policy.

"In less than a year the NCNP has become the rallying point for pacifists, campus radicals, leftwing crusaders, social theorists and Reform Democrats . . .

"To found the National Conference [Julian] Bond, [Simon] Casady, Stokely Carmichael of the Student Non-Violent Coordinating Committee (SNCC) and a host of militants assembled last August at the Santa Barbara, Cal., facilities of the Center for the Study of Democratic Institutions. . . .

". . . a second meeting [was] held immediately after last November's peace march on Washington. However, it was a third assembly of militants held last January in Chicago's McCormick Place that saw them joining with leaders of the Students for a Democratic Society (SDS) and the Committee for Independent Political Action (CIPA) to form the National Conference for New Politics."

"If Watts was wrong, we'd better go burn all the American history books."

That statement by co-chairman Dick Gregory was a keynote in the speech to the all-day organizing conference in Chicago, January 15, 1966, of the new nationwide Committee for Independent Political Action (CIPA).

The audience of more than 800 delegates applauded co-chairman Gregory's statement enthusiastically. They comprised leading members of organizations such as Voters of Illinois (an Affiliate of Americans for Democratic Action), Students for a Democratic Society, the American Friends Service Committee, Women for Peace, Student Non-Violent Coordinating Committee, and Southern Christian Leadership Conference, all joined in Leftist coalition with known Communists and race riot instigators with police records.

Most law-abiding Americans believe or hope that the criminal riot which took place in the Watts area of Los Angeles was an isolated incident in the past. To many delegates at the CIPA conference at McCormick Place, however, Watts was characteristic of the new "independent political action" described by several speakers as "people's politics."

The final plans for the strategy and tactics of several regional CIPA conferences, among which the Chicago conference ranked first in importance, had been made in secret sessions during Christmas weekend. As early as

December 9, 1965, however, Austin C. Wehrwein, *New York Times* correspondent in Chicago, reported:

"The first steps have been taken toward the formation of a political movement that would link civil rights, various student protests and opposition to the war in Vietnam, a policy statement disclosed today.

"An organization meeting has been called for Jan. 15.

"The policy statement said the election of candidates on 'an essentially radical program' was possible. . . .

"The organizers of the new united front include Paul Booth, national secretary of the Students for a Democratic Society; Dick Gregory, the Negro comedian; Tim Black, president of the Negro American Labor Council; Lutheran, Congregational and Roman Catholic clergymen active in civil rights; Prof. Robert Havighurst, a University of Chicago professor who wrote a report critical of the integration pace in Chicago schools; representatives of peace groups and representatives of Voters of Illinois, an affiliate of Americans for Democratic Action."

The policy statement of the Committee for Independent Political Action, dated December 10, 1965, stated

"It is now time to get a truly independent and anti-establishment political movement going. The undersigned feel that it is time to make the voice of independents felt at the ballot box. . . ."

OBJECTIVES ANALYZED

In the foregoing statement, "anti-establishment" means anti-U.S. Government as it presently exists, anti-capitalist, and anti-American as most Americans interpret our past and present economic, political and governmental traditions. The adjective "independent" means to be rid of restraints imposed by our existing laws and organizational authorities.

Signers of the CIPA policy declaration, several of whom have been long-time sponsors of Communist-front organizations, were:

Dr. Robert Havighurst	Rev. Bill Briggs
Lucy Montgomery	Lee Webb
Paul Booth	Earl Silbar

A.A. Rayner, Jr.
Ira Silbar
Rennie Davis
Paul Lauter
Father William Hogan
Rev. Harry Anderson
Richard Rothstein
Irving Birnbaum
John Kearney
Florence Scala
Lee Leibik

Ron Tabor
Dick Gregory
Sidney Lens
Timuel Black
Pat Devine
Henry Wineberg
Shirley Lens
Rev. Richard C. Knudsen
Jack Spiegel
Dr. Quentin Young

Co-chairmen of the CIPA organizing conference were Robert J. Havighurst, Professor of Education, University of Chicago, and Dick Gregory.

A record of Prof. Havighurst's long-time pro-Communist activities fills more than four pages (57-61) in the U.S. Government document "The Anti-Vietnam Agitation And The Teach-In Movement, The Problem of Communist Infiltration and Exploitation," issued by the Internal Security Subcommittee of the Senate Judiciary Committee, October 22, 1965.

On June 8, 1965, the *Chicago Tribune* reported:

"Comedian Dick Gregory was arrested last night in front of the Board of Education building . . . about four hours after he initiated round-the-clock vigils against the retention of Schools Supt. Benjamin Willis at the Board building and City Hall. . . .

"Gregory said demonstrators would stand at City Hall 24 hours a day 'until Willis gets out of office.' . . ."

The Senate Internal Security Subcommittee reported in its October 1965 document that the "so-called Vietnam Day Committee" had called for two days of nationwide protest against "American intervention in Vietnam," and that "Dick Gregory and Dave Dellinger" would speak at a rally in the Chicago Little Theater. The Subcommittee said the radical nature of the anti-Vietnam agitation was illustrated by the following statements in a flyer put out by the Vietnam Day Committee:

". . . we must turn to new tactics to affect American public opinion. We must put our bodies on the line. . . . If, for example, in Berkeley on October 16, thousands of students and others block the gates of the Oakland [California] Army Terminal where munitions are shipped to Vietnam, and are arrested, we think that attention will be focused dramatically on the issues. . . . Some thousands of middle-class youth being carried away by military police will be in every American living room. Controversy about these demonstrations will go on in churches and in poolrooms. . . . We will be in a better position to take the discussion about the war from the campus into the community."

In addition to co-chairmen Havighurst and Gregory, persons conducting the CIPA all-day conference in McCormick Place were listed as follows on the official program:

Convener: Irving Birnbaum
Speaker and Subject

Paul Lauter, Educator and AFSC Staff Worker—Political Perspectives.

James Bevel, Staff Director, SCLC Chicago Project—Community Organization.

Richard Rothstein,* National SDS, active JOIN Worker—The Student Movement in Chicago Politics.

Sidney Lens, Author, Lecturer and Peace Worker—The Linkage Between Peace, Civil Rights and Jobs.

Lawrence Landry, Nat'l Chairman, ACT; Leader, Chicago School Boycotts—Precinct Politics and Power.

Charlie Cobb, SNCC Field Secretary; Bond's Campaign Manager—The Implications of the Julian Bond Situation.

Monroe Sharp, Director, Chicago SNCC — Organizational Recommendations of Planning Committee.

Henry Wineberg, Chairman, Chicago Peace Council—Closing Remarks.

"There are new ways in which politics can be useful to us," said Paul Lauter, in his opening remarks to the CIPA

---

*Unable to appear, Mr. Rothstein was replaced as speaker by Robert Rossin of SDS.

delegates. "A guy in politics gets a lot of exposure. A lot of mystique attaches to him in a legal way."

Earlier, Mr. Lauter had issued a prospectus for independent politics in which he said that those wishing to achieve social, political and economic change have concentrated their energies on "direct action" protest activities and have not been heavily involved in electoral politics. He went on:

"Yet all over the country those in the 'liberal-radical' spectrum are turning with new vigor and hope and fresh ideas and techniques to independent electoral politics...

"To begin with, men and women devoted to an essentially radical program *can be elected.* John Conyers won a seat in Congress in Detroit despite strong opposition by establishment liberals. Julian Bond, long-time SNCC staff worker, was elected to the Georgia legislature last spring. ...

"Put another way, there have been creative relationships developed between Movement-style political protest and electoral political activity, and these can be expanded. ..."

"SHAKE AND DENT" AMERICAN GOVERNMENT

CIPA's initial aim—as set forth from the dais in McCormick Place—is "to scare, shake, dent and budge" the entire existing American governmental structure, from the White House to City Hall. This structure is "the establishment" opposed by the self-styled "liberal-radical" coalition.

An example of how the coalition can shake and dent the structure was cited by CIPA delegate Sylvia Woods during the conference morning discussion from the floor. Mrs. Woods boasted that as a political candidate in 1946, "I stole 10,000 votes from the machine in the election for legislature, even though I lost."

There is good reason for Sylvia Woods to say openly that she "stole" thousands of votes, for in 1946 most voters were ignorant of her real political affiliation. It was only in July 1947 that the *Chicago Tribune* carried the headline "LISTED LEADERS OF COMMUNISTS ARE WELL KNOWN" and the news:

"Most of the names of Illinois leaders of the Communist Party, listed yesterday before a Congressional committee hearing in Washington, are well known locally. Several of those named have run for office. . . .

"Sylvia Woods also ran for the legislature in 1946, although she was not announced as a Communist candidate. . . ."

At the CIPA organizing conference in Chicago, January 15, 1966, Mrs. Woods was elected to the 45-member executive committee along with two other well-known and Congressionally identified Communists—Fred Fine and Richard Criley.

"LIBERALS" JOIN REDS

In these days, when so much is being written and spoken by self-styled "liberals" in Americans for Democratic Action and the American Friends Service Committee about the dangers to our society of "extremism," it seems that skepticism concerning their sincerity is in order. For at the CIPA conference, "liberals" joined forces with Fred Fine and Richard Criley, whose Communist activities are so radical that the description "extremist" is an understatement.

On October 10, 1945, for example, the *Chicago Tribune* headlined "CIO UNION FIRES RED CONVICTED BY HEAVY VOTE—Accused of Violating Local, National Rules." The *Trib* story continued, "Richard L. Criley, former head of the Young Communist League of California and district educational director of the Congress of Industrial Organization, was expelled from local 28, United Packinghouse Workers (CIO) yesterday by a 59 to 6 vote of the membership. . . . Criley had been found guilty of being a Communist and violating provisions of the union and CIO constitutions."

Concerning Fred Fine, the *Chicago Tribune* carried on March 28, 1957, the headline: "STENCH BOMBS MARK DEBATE IN U. OF C. HALL" and the report: "Two stench bombs released in Mandel Hall of the University of Chicago last night enlivened a debate by two Socialists and one Communist . . . Speakers were Max Schactman . . . Mulford Sibley . . . and Fred Fine, a national committeeman of the

Communist Party, who is appealing a four-year prison sentence for membership in an organization advocating overthrow of the United States Government. . . ."

With the foregoing record of CIPA delegates, it is entirely understandable that the *Chicago Tribune* commented about the CIPA organizing conference in McCormick Place that the delegates couldn't agree "on what they hate most."

A HATE MEETING

The pervading emotion at the CIPA winter gathering was cold hatred. The only warmth in the assembly hall and meeting rooms came from the central heating plant in the enormous civic center. The cold hatred was like the white ice in Lake Michigan. Though many of the speakers talked "peace," several of them were militants preaching violence and extreme racism. These CIPA leaders' most despised "enemies" appear to be, in order of priority: the FBI, the police, the city, state and federal governments, the fire department.

"That's an FBI man over there," said a husky woman to a friend in a hallway. "We goin' to get us two, next summer. Just to show it can be done. They can be hurt the same as police."

Next summer. Next summer.

Spoken and repeated over and over, the phrase "next summer" grew more and more ominous at the CIPA meeting, like the somber beat of a bass kettledrum in a dirge.

A main speaker at the morning CIPA plenary session was Lawrence Landry, national chairman of ACT, an organization which, according to the press, was a main inciter of the 1965 summer Chicago riots in which scores of persons were injured, most of them innocent Negro bystanders. Tragically, a Negro woman bystander was killed by a hook-and-ladder fire truck that swerved out of control while responding to a false alarm. On August 14, the *Chicago Tribune* reported:

"Last night's violence [in which 62 persons were injured, including a ten year old girl, and 104 were arrested] broke out as ACT, a civil rights organization, held a rally near the fire station . . . in the racially tense neighborhood. ACT members passed out circulars denouncing white firemen for the accident in which the Negro woman was killed. Lawrence Landry, an organizer of the ACT group, spoke during the rally and told a swelling crowd, 'You are misused in a white-controlled society.' "

At the CIPA meeting, Lawrence Landry played a most important part. Not only was he a main speaker in the morning plenary session, but he also was chairman of a workshop session in the afternoon. A mimeographed working paper by him was distributed to all delegates. In a footnote to it, author Landry pointed out, "While this paper is designed for political action in the Negro ghetto, it is felt to be also applicable to work in lower-class white and ethnic communities."

Prior to the CIPA conference, the organizers had issued an instruction sheet in the form of "suggestions" for the conduct of the afternoon workshop sessions. These were managed mostly according to the Communist technique of "democratic centralism," with main decisions reached beforehand, then their announcement at the beginning of the session, next an alleged free speech discussion of the decisions, and finally a unanimous vote on their adoption.

Lawrence Landry opened the CIPA workshop of which he was chairman with the statement, "Power is something you have to take. I am here to talk about black power."

Nahaz Rogers, who acted as resource person for Landry in the workshop session, was a leader in the racial incitement that led to the 1965 riots in Chicago. In the session, Mr. Rogers said, "We are not here to do good. We are here to seize power. Don't ask us what we'll do with it when we get it. First we have to get it. The democratic process is a great thing, *but you don't come to the democratic process democratically.*"

Six months later, during the July 1966 Chicago riots by black youth gangs, riots that cost lives and heavy property damage, Pete Hamill of the *New York Post* reported under the headline "The Guerrillas" that Nahaz Rogers had been "meeting with the youth gang leaders for a year and a half, and was associated with Frederick (Doug) Andrews, a leader of the Chicago branch of RAM (Revolutionary Action Movement)." Mr. Hamill continued, "Last Friday, as the National Guard moved in, police raided Andrews' apartment, arrested him and a number of others, and said they had found plans for blowing up a suburban train, guns, and instructions for making Molotov cocktails."

Nahaz Rogers was closely connected with the organization "New Breed," a militant racist Black Nationalist movement. Several of its members later infiltrated the Republican Party in Illinois and were very active in Charles Percy's campaign for election to the U.S. Senate.

In the hallway outside the CIPA meeting rooms at McCormick Place, January 1966, I myself saw several extremely well dressed Negro delegates wearing registration badges with "New Breed" pencilled in below their names. One of them was in earnest conversation with a heavy set Negro wearing an orange jacket with the bluish-purple insignia "K.E.K." Reporters explained that this emblem was seen on some men's jackets during the Watts riot in Los Angeles, and that the letters stand for a brutally obscene anti-Semitic slogan reminiscent of those worn by Nazi ruffians during the Hitler regime. Frank Ditto, a black militant who had been arrested during the violent demonstrations in Chicago, was observed entering the CIPA workshop session headed by Lawrence Landry, and Ditto was nominated for the post of representative on the CIPA continuing committee by the Reverend William Baird, a participant in the Landry working session.

Immediately after the CIPA afternoon workshop sessions were concluded, the delegates assembled in the general meeting hall for a second plenary session. It was then that Dick Gregory made his speech.

"There are spies in this room," he alleged from the dais. "FBI spies and police spies and there's another spy I won't identify now, but we'll see about him later." Mr. Gregory did not explain why local and federal authorities would want to plant spies in an open all-day conference conducted for aboveboard political purposes. To those of us in the press up front near the dais, it seemed that either Mr. Gregory knew of behind-the-scenes CIPA activities warranting investigation by police authorities, or else he was making flagrantly demagogic and deliberately inflammatory anti-police propaganda.

Charles Cobb, field secretary of SNCC and campaign manager for Julian Bond in Georgia, was the next CIPA speaker. He explained that the main implication of the Julian Bond situation is that a "liberal-radical" coalition can penetrate and organize a constituency for victory at the polls and thus demonstrate the validity of people's politics techniques.

NO LACK OF FUNDS

Evidently there was no lack of funds for CIPA. Sidney Lens, a main speaker and member of the executive committee, told the delegates, "Don't worry. We can get the money to support our candidates. What we need most is the people to go out and work for them."

The Senate Internal Security Subcommittee published the following comments about Sidney Lens, October 22, 1965, in its staff study "The Anti-Vietnam Agitation and the Teach-In Movement" (pp. 65, 66):

"The name of Sidney Lens is listed as a supporter of the National Teach-In on the Vietnam War. . . . He is listed as a labor union official and author. He appeared as a witness before the Senate Internal Security Subcommittee on February 15, 1963. . . .

"Mr. Lens testified he was part of the visiting group of trade unionists to the Soviet Union [1960] and that he was director of the United Service Employees of Local 329 in Chicago at the time.

"Mr. Lens was actively interested in another Communist country, namely Cuba. He testified that he had made two trips to that country, that he had conferred with Fidel Castro and 'Ché' Guevara; that he had authorized the use of his name on an advertisement launching the Fair Play for Cuba Committee appearing in *The New York Times* of April 6, 1960; and that he acted as a speaker at meetings arranged by the Fair Play for Cuba Committee in Chicago . . .and in Los

Jerry Rubin, a bearded, barechested yippie leader, holds a toy M-16 rifle as he arrives in Washington, D.C., to appear before the House Committee on Un-American Activities 10/1/68. Rubin, a leader of the Youth International Party, described himself as the "guerrilla of the future." The committee was investigating street disorders during Democratic National Convention at Chicago in August, 1968.   UPI

Angeles [1960 and 1961]. Testimony before the Senate Internal Security Subcommittee on January 10, 1961, disclosed that the Fair Play for Cuba Committee had, from its inception, been subsidized by the Cuban Government.

"The Revolutionary Workers League has been cited as subversive by the [U.S.] Attorney General. In testimony before the ... Subcommittee ... on February 15, 1963, Sidney Lens invoked the Fifth Amendment in refusing to answer all questions pertaining to his connections with the Revolutionary Workers League. . . ."

When Mr. Lens confidently assured the CIPA organizing conference in McCormick Place, Chicago, January 15, 1966, "Don't worry. We can get the money to support our candidates," he gave no indication of where the money would come from. But it is a fact that he had no compunction about sponsoring a committee whose money came mostly from Fidel Castro's Communist regime.

On Sunday, January 23, 1966, *The New York Times Magazine* carried a sympathetic feature article by reporter John Corry on the notorious Staughton Lynd, then an assistant history professor at Yale University, and a leading figure at the First Annual Conference of Socialist Scholars, an organization reliably reported to be the radicals' brain trust for the new Committee for Independent Political Action. (Prof. Lynd defied U.S. passport regulations to go to Hanoi, North Vietnam, in company with Herbert Aptheker, leading theoretician of the Communist Party, U.S.A., and Thomas Hayden of Students for a Democratic Society.)

Reporter John Corry wrote that Lynd said about CIPA that this is the trend Lynd sees for American radicalism: independent candidates, provided the Left can eschew the factionalism of the 1930's, and "more desperate, more strident forms of action" if all else fails.

What could be "more desperate, more strident forms of action" than those taken by CIPA delegates in support of the bloody Watts and Chicago riots, and the violent civil disobedience at Berkeley, California?

What can be more strident and desperate liberal-radical coalition action than "anti-establishment" plots to destroy our FBI, police departments, city, state and federal administrations, and even the fire departments?

In August 1966, seven months after the CIPA conference in Chicago, the liberal-radical coalition formed at McCormick Place set up national headquarters in New York City for the newly-formed National Conference for New Politics (NCNP) and issued an appeal for campaign funds. The members of the NCNP national council were:

Paul Albert
California Democratic Council

Josiah Beeman V
National Committeeman, California Federation of Young Democrats

Paul Booth
National Council, Students for a Democratic Society

Samuel Bowles
Department of Economics, Harvard University

Robert Browne
Professor of Economics, Fairleigh-Dickinson University

Jane Buchenholz
Research Consultant

Stokely Carmichael
Chairman, Student Non-Violent Coordinating Committee

Grenville Clark
World Federalists

The Reverend William Sloane Coffin, Jr.
Chaplain, Yale University

Mrs. Gardner Cox
Civic Leader, Cambridge, Mass.

June Oppen Degnan
Publisher, *San Francisco Review*

Ronnie Dugger
Editor, *Texas Observer*

W.H. Ferry
Vice President, Center for the Study of Democratic Institutions

Gregory H. Finger
Sec'y—Acting Treas., National Conference for New Politics

Erich Fromm
Psychoanalyst

Edward P. Gottlieb
War Resisters League

Victoria Gray
Mississippi Freedom Democratic Party

Dick Gregory
Civil Rights Leader

Jerome Grossman
Chairman, Massachusetts Political Action for Peace

Alfred Hassler
Executive Secretary, Fellowship of Reconciliation

Nat Hentoff
Critic

Thomas Francis Hill
Past National Director, Catholic Council for Civil Liberties

Warren Hinckle
Executive Editor, *Ramparts Magazine*

Hallock Hoffman
Secretary-Treasurer, Center for the Study of Democratic Institutions

Mark De Wolfe Howe
Professor of Law, Harvard University

Richard Hudson
War/Peace Report

H. Stuart Hughes
Professor of History, Harvard University

Byron L. Johnson
Former Congressman, Colorado

Irving F. Laucks
Consultant, Center for Study of Democratic Institutions

Sidney Lens
Director Emeritus, Chicago Local, 329 Building Service Employees International Union

Herbert Marcuse
Professor of Philosophy, University of California, San Diego

Lenore Marshall
Poet

Frances McAllister
National Board, Friends Committee on Legislation

Carey McWilliams
Journalist

Stewart Meacham
Peace Education Secretary, American Friends Service Committee

Seymour Melman
Professor of Industrial Engineering, Columbia University

Everett Mendelsohn
Professor of the History of Science, Harvard University

Mrs. Kenneth Montgomery
Civic Leader, Chicago, Illinois

Barrington Moore, Jr.
Russian Research Center, Harvard University

Paul O'Dwyer
Former New York City Councilman

Martin Peretz
Committee on Social Studies, Harvard University

Gifford Phillips
State Finance Committee, California Democratic Party

Sumner Rosen
American Federation, State, County & Municipal Employees Union

Don Rothenberg
Californians for Liberal Representation

Marshall Sahlins
Professor of Anthropology, University of Michigan

Michael Schneider
San Francisco Director, California Democratic Council

Robert Schwartz
National Board, Committee for a Sane Nuclear Policy

Robert B. Silvers
Editor, *New York Review of Books*

Pitirim Sorokin
Past President, American Sociological Association

Benjamin Spock, M.D.
Pediatrician

William Strickland
Executive Director, Northern Student Movement

Albert Szent-Gyorgi, M.D.
Nobel Laureate

Harold Taylor
Past President, Sarah Lawrence College

Monroe S. Wasch
American Federation, State, County & Municipal Employees Union

Arthur I. Waskow
Senior Fellow, Institute for Policy Studies

Lee Webb
Student Leader

Peter Weiss
Executive Committee, Benjamin Franklin Reform Democrats

Henry J. Wineberg
Committee for Independent Political Action—Chicago

Michael P. Wood
U.S. National Student Association

"LIBERAL" — RADICAL INTERLOCK

Study of the NCNP national council shows there was a definite political-intellectual interlock among personnel in the Center for the Study of Democratic Institutions and CIPA-NCNP and the radical *Ramparts* magazine.

Stanley K. Sheinbaum was on the staff at the Center, on the Board of Editors of *Ramparts* magazine, and was active in CIPA-NCNP politics.

Arthur I. Waskow was on the national council for CIPA-NCNP, was a contributing editor to *Ramparts*, and is both an author for and frequent participator in the Center at Santa Barbara.

Robert Scheer is an author for and participant in the Center, a member of the Board of Editors of *Ramparts,* and was active in CIPA-NCNP politics.

The revolutionary aim of all these festering radical-extremist minorities is being furthered again and again in many of the smoothly presented "occasional papers" published by the Center at Santa Barbara. Expensively printed and well edited, these papers appear to be innocuous intellectual studies couched in erudite language. Actually, they are revolutionary or anarchic documents written in Aesopian language designed to ensnare the reader. But any reader with patience and discernment can get the point.

Here is the point of the Center's August 1966 occasional paper, "The Rise and Fall of Liberal Democracy" by Harvey Wheeler, who was co-author of the novel *Fail Safe:*

".... America has outlived the participational democracy of her fathers. She must quickly bring forth a new one... Our times demand the development of new conceptions of legislation and new processes of deliberation...

"Are there any signs of such a development? Recently a new doctrine of democracy has appeared. It was developed initially by young people in their twenties, but despite its adamant youth-centered bias, leadership of the movement is exercised by those already in their thirties. The 'Port Huron Statement' of the Students for a Democratic Society, now only four years old, has already assumed the status of a holy text. Its framers, meaning to turn their backs on the ideological squabbles of the 1930's, seized upon a few simple propositions. Their overriding devotion was given to what they call *participatory* democracy. This not only referred to anti-organization principles for conducting business of the movement itself but also expressed a new approach to working with the unrepresented or dispossessed members of society. The Establishment, standing in the way of participatory democracy, is the announced enemy. There is no real difference between the Establishment liberals and the Establishment conservatives, between the civil and the corporate elites. Indeed, liberalism's unshakable hold on political and industrial power makes *it* the more formidable adversary. The solution? Organize the unrepresented, activate the poor and the Negroes, reconstitute the discontented, form a new coalition committed to the building of a new society dedicated to democracy, world order, and civil and economic justice."

Harvey Wheeler says this "new coalition" of the "protest movement" recapitulates Thomas Jefferson's pattern for America. It always has been characteristic of the Left in our country—whether Old Left or New Left—that it obeys the earliest command of the Communist Party, U.S.A., when it was first created, to regard the American Revolution of 1776 as only the "first" revolution in our country, and to regard the names of the Founding Fathers as useful tools for promoting the Red Revolution in America.

To bring about the "second revolution," one controlled by the Leftist minority, is the basic aim of the liberal-radical coalition in our country, a coalition using the slogan "new politics."

Chapter 4

OPEN ADVOCACY OF VIOLENCE

WHILE ORDINARY TRAVELERS from out of town were registering at the reception desk in the main lobby of the Hotel Commodore in New York City, Friday evening, September 9, 1966, more than two thousand members of the Old and New Left were registering at tables set up in ballroom floor hallways to attend the Second Annual Conference of Socialist Scholars.

The New Left movement in our country is generally described by misinformed or misleading members of the press as a spontaneous, amorphous grouping of rebellious youth. It is not. Any non-Socialist who attended the evening and daytime panel sessions of the Socialist Scholars during the week-end of September 9-11, would have been forced to recognize, as did I, that most members of the New Left are activists instigated, controlled and manipulated by disciplined members of the Communist Party working in a united front with Marxist ideologues.

NEWS MEDIA IGNORE REVEALING SESSIONS

Was it to foster illusion or misconception that the big press—the wire services, broadcasting networks, big circulation magazines and newspapers—stayed away from the conference? It is hard to find a satisfactory explanation of why they granted it privileged sanctuary in the East Ballroom and West Ballroom of the Hotel Commodore in the center of the city.

There were no TV cameras to film the arrival from London of white-bearded radical Marxist zealot Isaac Deutscher, invited by the Socialists to open their conference with a discourse "On Socialist Man." Nor were there any cameras turned on 54-year-old Victor Perlo, identified in Congressional hearings as a member of a Soviet espionage ring while he was a U.S. Government employee during World War II. No well-known reporter was present to interview conference panelist Communist Herbert Aptheker, then age 51, and running for Congress in Brooklyn, N.Y.

For some inexplicable reason it seems that nowadays our communications media personnel report graphically only on the effects of the Leftist radicals' activities—on the bloody race riots, street demonstrations, disrupting and costly acts of civil disobedience—but stay away from the gatherings where plans for such activities are hatched, though most meetings, as this one was, are publicly announced.

There was not an empty chair in the 800-seat Windsor Ballroom at the Commodore when the Socialist teachers and their radical Leftist audience gathered to hear Polish-born Isaac Deutscher of London. He was introduced by Prof. H. H. Wilson of Princeton University, who described Mr. Deutscher as "a contributor to *The Economist* and *The Observer.*" That is a fact, though most Deutscher articles in those publications were unsigned.

When Deutscher went to the rostrum, the audience stood to honor him; they did so again after his address.

The essence of Deutscher's speech was extreme Marxism-Leninism in its original Bolshevik form.

It seemed preposterous that an audience in 1966 could listen to such evil tripe without bursting into derisive laughter turning into catcalls of indignant repudiation.

WOULD ABOLISH FAMILY

Yet it became clear, during subsequent panel sessions of the Socialist conference, that the New Leftist radicalism of today is in no way different from the Old Bolshevism of half a century ago. To anyone believing that the family as a social unit is essential to maintenance of a decent society, there was little difference between Isaac Deutscher's call, September 9, 1966, for "complete freedom of sexual life that will abolish the family," and Brooklyn Polytechnic Asst. Professor of Economics Shane Mage's call from the same dais for youth to follow today the advice of convicted marijuana handler Timothy Leary (ousted from the Harvard faculty) to "turn on, tune in, drop out" through use of the hallucinogenic drug LSD and marijuana. Nor was there substantial difference between Deutscher's call for "destruction of the monogamic bourgeois family as we know it," and the statements in a paper read for 70-year-old Prof. Herbert Marcuse (unable to attend because he was at a Communist meeting in Prague) of the University of California in San Diego. After having declared "the Marxian idea of socialism is not radical enough," Prof. Marcuse urged, "We must develop the moral-sexual rebellion of the youth."

USE OF LSD URGED

When dark-haired Prof. Shane Mage, speaking in a nasal voice with Adam's apple twitching in his thin throat, urged the young people present to take LSD in order "to create a free society," neither white-bearded Isaac Deutscher nor any Socialist professor from Yale, Princeton, Columbia or non-Ivy League university rose to utter a word of protest against this deliberate corruption of the young. Yet only a few days earlier, there had appeared in the press everywhere an official warning against LSD by the International Association of Chiefs of Police who called for international legislation against its non-medical use.

Just how much stress the Socialist teachers and their activist pupils in the New Left place on use of LSD as a means of breaking down middle-class customs and morality may be seen in the text of the Radical Education Project (REP) document sponsored by Students for Democratic Action. Many SDS leaders were present at the conference and their REP document was widely circulated there. It urges a study of the questions: "Are all existing instances of private enterprise antithetical to our values? How do we relate to riots? to the sexual revolution? to pornography? to LSD? . . ."

Disdaining "bourgeois" manners and culture, the young radicals in REP and dozens of other Leftist groups in the ballroom at the Commodore gave rapt attention to aging Marxist-Leninist-Trotskyite Deutscher as he said "Socialist man will be exempt from worship and awe." After fatherhood has come to be regarded only as biological, and "paternal authority" as a mere social institution to be gotten rid of, then the "bourgeois form of the patriarchal family" will be obliterated, and infants brought up "in a communal nursery, after the destruction of the family as we know it, will be free of aggressive tendencies."

In what the Socialists describe as "the transition period to revolution," it appears, however, that the family as we know it, well fed on the good fruits of free enterprise, plays today a most helpful role in aiding the authors of its destruction.

Afterwards, in the hallway outside the East Ballroom, a Socialist teacher stressed the importance of leading the bourgeoisie on toward suicide. "Only the clunks stay in the clink," he said. "Fortunately—as at Berkeley, for example—the parents of middle class and wealthy students in our movement bail them out."

A fat male "clunk" with shoulder-length hair, thick beard, leather jacket, laced boots and filthy fingernails shoved a mimeographed sheet into the Ivy League Socialist's hand.

I received one, too. It read:

"The John Brown Coordinating Committee, deeply concerned with the growing violence of the attacks by the White Power structure on the developing militant black peoples movement as exemplified by recent attacks in Chicago and the arrest of Stokely Carmichael in Atlanta urge participants in the Socialist Scholars Conference to stage a march from—Hotel Commodore to Rockefeller Plaza—time—5:30 p.m.—to demonstrate our concern and solidarity with the Afro-American people and against white supremacy."

The "clunk" put a hand on the Socialist professor's arm. "You with us?" The professor smiled, said a noncommittal "maybe," and turned ingratiatingly to a good looking young man with short cut smooth black hair, blue eyes, clean shaven face and a neat navy blue suit. "How are things at Yale?" said the professor. "You're a student of Woodward's, aren't you?"

The "Woodward" referred to is Prof. C. Vann Woodward of Yale University who, on Sunday afternoon in the Windsor Ballroom, described himself as "a liberal," but began his discussion of an inter-Socialist controversy between Communist Herbert Aptheker and Prof. Eugene D. Genovese with the statement, "I identify with Aptheker."

CARMICHAEL THEIR HERO

All during the discussion in the Commodore over the week-end, it was obvious that Stokely Carmichael of the Student Non-Violent Coordinating Committee—jailed in Atlanta on a charge of "inciting to riot"—was the revolutionary hero. Mention of his name during panel or floor discussion brought loud cheers and crashing applause. There was talk by some Socialist intellectuals and youth group leaders in various radical organizations of "running a radical ticket in 1968—Staughton Lynd for President, and Stokely for Vice President." One of the youth leaders explained, "Not that we'd expect to get any big amount of votes—but it would give us entry into places on and off campus where we couldn't usually operate. It would be very useful for contacts-making."

Three main facts emerged clearly from the Second Annual Conference of Socialist Scholars in New York City, September 1966: (1) The American Marxists are abandoning their pretense of non-violence for open advocacy of violence; (2) they have successfully linked the American Marxist revolutionary movement with its counterparts throughout the world; (3) they are drunk with success and have cast away former caution about their real objectives.

At the discussion of "Poverty and Powerlessness," panelist James Haughton, director of the Harlem Unemployment Center, ranted into the microphone on the dais, after Prof. Richard A. Cloward of Columbia University had branded our welfare system in our welfare state as "lawless":

"Specifically, yes, the welfare system is rotten, but so is the whole American system rotten, You can't look any where in this country and see any thing but rottenness. . . .

"We must pinpoint the enemy of poor people—American imperialism. Wherever the American octopus reaches out its tentacles, there you will find exploitation, cruelty, poverty, mass impoverishment."

Dr. Haughton called for "revolutionary change, not reforms," and he predicted that "the black Uncle Tom flunkies, like those in the NAACP and Urban League, will ultimately be kicked out."

Dr. Haughton said, "We had a march against the war in Vietnam, and we got some data from Prof. Melman (Seymour D., Professor of Industrial Engineering) at Columbia University. I've been in touch with him and put his conclusions in fact sheets to workers."

Dr. Haughton said Prof. Melman had told him the dollar would be devalued in 1967 and 25 per cent of the Negro people would be unemployed. Dr. Haughton continued, "Then those people in the Administration will learn about riots in the streets. They rioted in the 1930's, but that won't be anything compared to '67!"

The applause in the ballroom was deafening.

CONTACTS WITH GUERRILLAS ABROAD

The kind of citizenship admired by the Socialists was depicted by James Petras of the Free Speech Movement at the University of California at Berkeley, who described to the conference audience his recent voyages to Latin America, his contacts with Marxist and Communist revolutionary forces there. Petras said that in Latin America today, "revolutionary guerrilla warfare in the countryside fosters citizenship."

All during the Commodore conference, many Socialist leaders and members of the audience talked openly about their direct contacts with guerrilla warfare leaders in Asia, Africa and Latin America. They discussed recent visits to Havana, Hanoi, Moscow, Prague and other Red capitals.

Like many citizens, I have puzzled over how young campus radicals and academicians manage to travel from

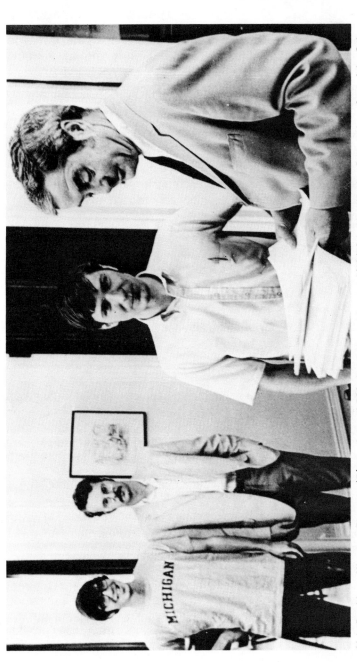

Yale President, Kingman Brewster (R), receives a 1,500 signature petition on 4/29/70 in New Haven, Connecticut, from John Cole, class of '71, supporting his statements questioning whether Black Panthers can get a fair trial. UPI

continent to continent with the greatest of ease, often in defiance of State Department regulations and of Passport Division security provisions. At the Second Annual Conference of Socialist Scholars, I learned how they do it.

The young radicals travel along the smooth rails of an underground campus shuttle system that transports them, armed with highest academic credentials given by sponsoring Socialist professors, from California to Tanzania, from Michigan to guerrilla camps in Peru and Chile, from Massachussetts to African bush rebel enclaves in Mozambique and Angola. Often the bills are footed by tax-exempt foundations.

Robert Fitch, a young radical present at the conference, told friends on Saturday morning, "I have an appointment Monday morning with someone in the Department of African Affairs at New York University to arrange for a trip to Mozambique to see Mondlane."

"Wonderful", they said.

Dr. Eduardo Mondlane is head of the pro-Communist Mozambique Liberation Front.

RADICAL INTELLIGENCE NETWORK

On Sunday afternoon there took place in the West Ballroom a meeting of leaders in the Radical Education Project (REP), an enterprise of Students for a Democratic Society. REP, with headquarters at Ann Arbor,Michigan, sent out a letter, August 18, 1966, which stated:

"The Socialist Scholars Conference looms as a significant event in the development of the Left in America."

The letter was accompanied by an outline of REP projects, including an "International Intelligence Network" described as:

". . .a network of people in the U.S. and abroad, closely tuned to international events, who will serve the movement as quick, incisive sources of intelligence. . . . Such a network, including scholars, journalists, leftist youth leaders, government officials [sic!], guerrilla leaders, etc., can provide us with first hand reports and analysis of the action of insurgent movements, the workings of the foreign policy apparatus, kinds of impending developments. ... Already we have contacts in Japan, most European countries, Canada, and with Guatemalan guerrillas, Vietnamese rebels and neutrals, African nationalist, and others. These contacts are being extended, and to them we must add American scholars with specialized knowledge and contacts. ... By maintaining regular correspondence with radical groups and scholars abroad, we can increase the degree of coordination between their work and that of the American movement."

On reading the foregoing, I understood how it happened that Communists parading in the Place Bruckère on May Day in Brussels, 1965, and "Peace Parade" marchers along Fifth Avenue in New York City 1966, carried identical hideous effigies of Uncle Sam, identical banners and placards, shouted identical slogans in Flemish, French and English.

The Second Annual Conference of Socialist Scholars showed conclusively that the American campus-based radical international intelligence network exists and is a menacing threat to the internal and external security of the United States. I wish some high-ranking members of our judiciary had been present to hear the Socialist leaders discuss their "five year plan" to cooperate with "national revolutionary liberation wars" in three continents to put "unbearable strain" on the U.S. Government "to bring it down." Perhaps our judiciary would be more sympathetic with the State Department's effort to restrict the jaunts abroad of American subversives, and to enforce the passport regulations necessary for protection of our country.

I understand fully now why the Leftists have battled so hard in our courts for what they describe as "the right to travel."

RADICAL "PROGRESS"

Prof. Gaylord LeRoy of Temple University urged on the youth of the New Left the necessity to study "more seriously the advances made by the Socialist countries of the world."

The kind of "advances" promoted by the Socialist teachers in our own country—with not a single objection voiced from dais or ballroom floor— was enough to send shivers down the spine of any American devoted to law, order and decent morality. In the Sunday afternoon Windsor Ballroom panel session on "The Legacy of Negro Slavery," the main paper was delivered by Prof. Eugene D. Genovese of Rutgers. He urged on American Negroes a policy of black nationalism. In the course of his remarks, Prof. Genovese talked about Karl Marx' theory of surplus value and said, "We ought to be delighted every time a worker steals something from his plant."

Though Genovese's fellow panelist Communist Herbert Aptheker opposed the policy of black nationalism, and called for Negro-White radical unity, he agreed with Prof. Genovese's point of view on theft. "There is a whale of difference," said Aptheker, "between the stealing by a worker and the wholesale stealing by General Motors."

The inter-Socialist dispute over Black Nationalism versus Negro-White radical unity was fairly sharp but not really antagonistic.

At the business meeting in the East Ballroom, Sunday afternoon, Paul Sweezy, gray-haired editor of the radical *Monthly Review* and member of the steering committee, commented on "the amazing progress we have made since our First Conference at Columbia, last September, progress far beyond our expectations."

Tired and dizzy with dismay, I shut my eyes. It seemed the ballroom floor was sliding from beneath me, the ceiling was about to fall, the walls were crumbling. Yes, indeed, the Socialist Scholars and New Left made amazing progress in America after their first meeting: LSD extolled in *Playboy* by a man found guilty in court of transporting marijuana, fined $30,000 and sentenced to 30 years' imprisonment; LSD "art" lauded in *Life*; race riots and bloodshed in Cleveland, Chicago, Atlanta, Brooklyn, Baltimore; a witness before a committee of the United States Senate boasting of his eight illegitimate children by different mothers.

"Nihilism", said Nietzsche in the late 19th century, "is for the supreme values to be rendered worthless." He predicted nihilism would prevail during the 20th and 21st centuries.

The remembered sound of Isaac Deutscher's thick Polish-accented English with an Oxonian overlay was again in my ears and they hurt with the echo of his call for "the destruction of the monogamic bourgeois family as we know it."

Though the air-conditioning was blowing cool air into the ballroom, the atmosphere grew more and more oppressive—heavy and ominous as before a storm.

WORK OF A FEW "INTELLECTUALS"

I gripped the sides of a straight chair to steady myself. How right Hermann Rauschning was, I thought, having recently studied his *The Revolution of Nihilism* (1939) and *The Redemption of Democracy* (1941) in which he explained, better than almost any other author, how the Russian and German people fell prey to Marxism-Leninism and Hitlerism. He showed that Communism and National Socialism were only symptoms of a world revolution in which a few intellectuals pretend to be able to create "a new society" in order to seize totalitarian power over the masses.

Quietly, I made my way through the crowded aisle in the ballroom. It seemed I was being swept away into the crashing cacophony of the finale in Maurice Ravel's symphonic work "La Valse," the most prophetic artistic creation of the 20th century, in which dancers sway gladly to the rhythm of a waltz in a ballroom with mirrors, candelabra, and doors opening into formal gardens, but are caught in an inexorable force whirling faster and faster until the floor vanishes beneath their feet, the mirrors splinter, the doors fly off their hinges in the gusts of a terrible wind, and nothing remains but destruction and chaos.

Is this to be the fate of our society, of the American way of life? If the Socialist teachers and the New Left have their way, it will be.

Chapter 5

WELFARE OVERLOAD

...Promoted to Disrupt U.S.

MORE THAN ANY other Socialist Scholar, it is Professor Richard A. Cloward, of the Columbia University School of Social Work, who, during the last four years, has adversely affected the pocketbook of every American taxpayer through promoting a welfare strategy which is, in reality, a conspiracy. Its aim is to bring down our present form of government by putting an insupportable welfare "overload" on local, state and federal budgets, an overload creating the demand for a guaranteed annual income.

Dr. Cloward, along with an assistant, Dr. Frances Piven, originally put forth his welfare strategy in an article for the radical Leftist weekly *The Nation,* May 2, 1966. Four months later, he further developed the strategy in a paper presented to the Second Annual Conference of Socialist Scholars in New York City.

In their article for *The Nation*, Cloward-Piven wrote "it is not generally known that for every person on the [welfare] rolls at least one more probably meets existing criteria of eligibility but is not obtaining assistance." They said that to remedy the "discrepancy" would precipitate "a profound financial and political crisis." Wanting to create exactly that, Drs. Cloward and Piven proposed "a massive drive to recruit the poor *onto* the welfare rolls." Such recruitment, plus help to welfare recipients in getting fullest possible benefits under the letter of the welfare laws, would produce—wrote Cloward-Piven—"bureaucratic disruption in local and state governments."

At a time when all responsible government leaders were trying hard in 1966 to create understanding among Americans, Socialist Scholars Cloward and Piven were striving to create the opposite and wrote in *The Nation:*

"A welfare crisis would, of course, produce dramatic local political crisis, disrupting and exposing rifts among urban groups. Conservative Republicans are always ready to declaim the evils of public welfare, and they would probably be the first to raise a hue and cry. But deeper and politically more telling conflicts would take place within the Democratic coalition: Whites—both working class ethnic groups and many in the middle class—would be aroused against the ghetto poor, while liberal groups, which until recently have been comforted by the notion that the poor are few and, in any event, receiving the beneficent assistance of public welfare, would probably support the movement. Group conflict, spelling political crisis for the local party apparatus, would thus become acute as welfare rolls mounted and the strains on local budgets became more severe. In New York City, where the Mayor is now facing desperate revenue shortages, welfare expenditures are already second only to those for public education. . . .

"It should also be noted that welfare costs are generally shared by local, state and federal governments, so that the crisis in the cities would intensify the struggle over revenues that is chronic in relations between cities and states. . . ."

TOWARD "DICTATORSHIP OF THE POOR AND THE MINORITIES"

What, basically, is the two Socialist Scholars' motive for creating conflict and crisis? As modern Marxists, they are well aware of the relative immunity of the American proletariat (i.e., the industrial factory workers) to Leftist radicalism. Therefore Cloward and Piven seek to create a United Socialist States of America by means other than classical dictatorship of the proletariat. They believe they can create such an America through dictatorship of "the poor and the minorities." In May 1966, Cloward-Piven spelled it out: "Since radical movements in America have rarely been able to provide visible economic incentives, they have usually failed to secure mass participation of any kind. ... If organizers can deliver millions of dollars in cash benefits to the ghetto masses, it seems reasonable to expect that the masses will deliver their loyalties to their benefactors."

At the Second Annual Conference of Socialist Scholars in New York City, September 1966, Dr. Cloward expatiated on the Cloward-Piven strategy, Dr. Piven added her own impromptu verbal comments and they both made plain their desire to replace the existing American system of government with a Marxist one.

When a member of the audience went to the floor microphone during the question period to ask whether Dr. Cloward's strategy is a substitute for "Socialist organization of the proletariat, the industrial factory workers," Dr. Frances Piven replied from the dais: "I really only want to make one point—the disruption of the system. Welfare rolls will begin to go up; welfare payments will begin to go up—the impact will be very, very sharp. The mounting welfare budget will increase taxes, force cities to turn to the federal government. We have to help people to make claims; for this they will organize and act."

Prof. Cloward explained that each welfare client in New York City was entitled under existing law to special benefits for clothing, blankets, etc. He said that in 1965 city special benefits welfare payments amounted to "about $40 per client" and he called for each welfare client to demand $100 to $1,000 in such benefits. He said there were 550,000 welfare clients in the city, but that by 1967 there probably would be 600,000.

Dr. Cloward said he had consulted with legal experts and "we estimate that $200 million in special grants" could be obtained in New York City alone. Dr. Cloward said that in early August, he himself had taken part in "a national conference to organize the welfare recipients movement." Dr. Cloward said he personally had taken part in Wednesday night meetings with welfare clients "week after week, month after month," and that as a result, "Next Monday there will be a demonstration of welfare recipients at City Hall."

He was a prophet of sharpest vision, as TV watchers soon found out.

The demonstration took place on schedule and was so violent that the police had to call for emergency reinforcements.

The big press coverage of the welfare recipients' demonstration at City Hall was at the wrong time in the wrong place. NBC and CBS cameras should have been focused on Prof. Richard A. Cloward as he read his paper in the ballroom at the Commodore. The TV newscasters would have gotten a beat on news about to burst into print. And if the U.S. Attorney General had been present at the Second Annual Conference of Socialist Scholars, he might have obtained most useful information about who are the real agitators in our midst.

POVERTY PROGRAM HONEYCOMB FOR LEFTISTS

Though Dr. Cloward is bent on causing the worst kind of racial and civic trouble, he was extremely influential in poverty programs set up during the Kennedy and Johnson Administrations. He was research director in the scandal-ridden Mobilization for Youth Program, a multimillion dollar pilot project (set up in 1962 with federal, city and Ford Foundation funds) for the future multi-billion dollar War on Poverty. In summer 1964, the *New York Daily News* reported, "Mobilization for Youth, Inc., . . . is under intensive federal-city investigation as a suspected Red honeycomb for leftists who have used its facilities—and juveniles—to foment rent strikes and racial disorders." A week later, the *New York Times* reported, "A Federal Bureau of Investigation loyalty check on personnel in Mobilization for Youth has shown that the agency has two employes who are current members of the Communist Party and three who belong to other leftist organizations. In addition, the F.B.I. report . . . will say that at least 32 of the agency's employes have been linked in the past to the Communist Party or front groups."

Mobilization for Youth, with Dr. Cloward as research director, operated in the Lower East Side of Manhattan. "The first persons to cry 'foul!' were the landlords of the area," reported Newton H. Fulbright in *U.S.A. Magazine* during the summer of 1964.

"Foul!" is the least that city landlords will cry as Socialist Scholars Cloward and Piven, and the Citywide Coordinating Committee of Welfare Groups, and the National Welfare Rights Organization carry out their disruptive plans. More than likely, the mayors and welfare commissioners will cry "Conspiracy!", as did New York City Commissioner of Social Services Jack R. Goldberg when, on November 8, 1968, welfare recipients — goaded by Dr. Cloward and his associates — spent their rent money on other things and deliberately sought eviction by landlords.

On November 11, 1968, the *Chicago Tribune* said in a powerful editorial entitled "The Conspiracy Progresses":

"We have already pointed out that New York's welfare rights movement, which is now taking the form of a rent strike, is a fraudulent scheme perpetrated on the theory that by overthrowing the present welfare structure the poor will somehow come out better off than they are now. Just how they can find security in chaos, or how they will be protected from cleverer and greedier marauders, is never explained.

"But the broader and more frightening aspect of the welfare rights movement is that it has been deliberately planned by a handful of Socialist Scholars as part of a national rebellion manifested also in peace marches, race riots, campus demonstrations, and attacks on 'bourgeois morality.' . . .

"Thus a uniform pattern emerges. The welfare militants, like the campus militants and the black militants, are calling, in effect, for secession. They are trying to pull the social structure apart, group by group, until it collapses in chaos—which won't help the blacks or the poor or the students but is just what the radical leaders thrive on."

If Commissioner Goldberg and Human Resources Commissioner Mitchell Ginsberg and Mayor John V. Lindsay had been at the meeting held at Broadway United Church of Christ, New York City, on November 6, 1968, they would have found out a great deal about the welfare "conspiracy"—how it works and who is in it.

A University of Wisconsin student finishes ripping down the American Flag from a U.S. Post Office during an anti-General Electric Co. protest on 2/12/70 in Madison, Wisconsin. GE was on campus interviewing prospective employees. Eight persons were arrested and many windows broken during the demonstration. UPI

HOW THE CONSPIRACY WORKS

The meeting was attended by "coordinators" belonging to the Citywide Coordinating Committee of Welfare Groups, and they conspired there with welfare recipients, male and female, white and black, with lawyers and law students, to break the law. Their actions have been graphically reported in the press. "Swarms of militant welfare clients, most of them women," reported the N.Y. *Daily News* in October 1968, "invaded the welfare centers in Brooklyn, Bronx, Queens and Staten Island. . . . overturning desks and hurling telephones out the windows of the offices." On September 18, United Press International reported from St. Joseph, Michigan, "Four persons were arrested and two policemen injured Wednesday in a purse-swinging, fist-pounding scuffle when welfare mothers invaded the Berrien County courthouse. . . . An estimated 50 aid-to-dependent-children mothers. . . . picketed welfare offices in the basement of the building and blocked entrances to the offices with a 'human wall' ".

At Broadway United Church of Christ, November 6, there were at least 50 "coordinators" teaching "recruits" (as they call them) how to organize for illegal action and how to commit it. The coordinators' ideological tutors are Prof. Cloward and Dr. Piven; their director in the City-wide Committee is Hulbert James; their chairman in New York City is Beulah Sanders, a Negro "welfare mother" whose loud rantings before the Democratic National Committee in August 1968 scandalized Chairman Hale Boggs and millions of television viewers.

PLANT AGITATORS IN CROWDS

Mrs. Sanders and a white woman group leader discussed the Cloward-Piven planned rent revolt for December 1968, and also a program to disrupt Christmas shopping at several big department stores. At Beulah Sanders' invitation, a Negro welfare mother "coordinator" instructed her sister and brother conspirators, white and black, on how to carry out the December "shop-in."

"You recruit people on welfare to go pick out what they want—about a hundred dollars worth," she explained, "and go to the cash register at May's or Macy's or Abraham & Straus. First you demand a discount. They won't give it to you. Meantime, you're holding up the store's business. When the cashier demands that you pay, you say 'Charge it to Welfare.' This will start up a big argument. People with Christmas shopping will be waiting in line to pay at the cash register. We can drive a lot of angry customers away from the store. Meantime, the cashier has got to send for the manager. Before any new purchases can be rung up, the whole register has got to be gone over. The customers get madder and madder. The store calls for the police. The cops come and we put up a struggle. Don't worry. We'll take care of the legal appeals when you get arrested. You put up a struggle and we'll get some people planted in the store to be very upset customers shocked at police brutality to welfare mothers just trying to get something for their kids for Christmas. You can bet Macy's and A&S owners will put the heat on the City to get us out of the place because it's bad for business and get the City to give us what we want. We'll raise such hell they'll charge you with creating a public nuisance. A few of you will be arrested and they'll let the rest go. Our friends that Cloward and Piven send us will take care of things. Just you take care of your angle and Columbia will take care of the legal angle. You try it and see. You'll get what you want."

It was fascinating, in a terrifying way, to hear the conspirators in the Broadway United Church plan to plant people acting as "very upset customers" among Christmas shoppers when welfare mothers tangle with police. The placing of *agents provocateurs* or professional actors playing the role of agitators in crowds is a sinister business.

At the conspiratorial coordinators' meeting in the Broadway church, November 6, there was a discussion of a December agitation program for welfare clients demanding a special "just for Xmas" allotment. "We can cause such a rumpus in crowds waiting to see Santa Claus that the City will be glad to hand it to us," said a coordinator.

A week later, Associated Press reported from Philadelphia:

"Welfare recipients, saying they want to 'provide a decent American Christmas for our children,' staged demonstrations at Department of Welfare offices here and in Chester today.

"There were about 500 women and children here and about 15 in Chester. They said they represented the Welfare Rights Organization and wanted adequate money to buy 'decent' presents for their children—not toys from 'thrift shops.' "

DIRE POSSIBILITIES OF RENT STRIKE

After the coordinators' discussion in Broadway United Church of Christ about demanding special Christmas allotments, "welfare mother" Beulah Sanders issued strict instructions to the group about a rent revolt. "We're going to concentrate on the month of December," she announced, "because the landlords won't be able to get themselves together in one month to take legal action." Another coordinator said, "Just you be sure to get your recruits to spend the December rent money for Christmas. You tell 'em: 'Just you spend it and get what you want.' You tell 'em: 'That's what Columbia wants you to do.' "

What Columbia, meaning, of course, Prof. Cloward and Dr. Piven, wanted the Citywide Coordinating Committee of Welfare Groups to do was made plain in the radical tabloid *New York Free Press* in the "RENT REVOLT" by Cloward-Piven. It stated:

"Aside from reasonable assurances that they will not be evicted, tenants need an incentive to strike. The rent money is such an incentive, but only if the tenant can pocket it or spend it. . . .

"The response of landlords and municipal housing agencies to a successful rent revolt will vary depending on local conditions. Where landlords have little equity in their buildings, many may simply abandon them. In other situations, landlords may try to wait out the strikers, exerting counter-pressure by turning off utilities and discontinuing services. But there is nothing a landlord can turn off that tenants can't turn back on. And if marshals can be successfully resisted, so can utility men threatening to turn off gas and electricity."

In describing the terrible conditions which might ensue as consequences of evictions during a rent revolt, Commissioner Jack Goldberg said it could "cause kids to freeze on the streets." It seems Cloward and Piven were aware of the dire possibilities, but were nevertheless hell-bent on creating a welfare rent crisis throughout the nation to arrive at a Marxist solution on the federal level. Their article "RENT REVOLT" went on to present truly macabre possibilities at which they did not even faintly shudder. They stated:

"When landlords terminate services or abandon the buildings, tenants may want to take over the task of providing minimum services. If they have the organizational capability to do so, they can then settle down to rent-free living . . .

"But if a neighborhood does not or cannot take over the servicing of buildings, the consequences might turn into a *political advantage* [italics added] for the strikers. Under such circumstances, dangerous conditions would quickly develop: hazards to health, threats of fire, the spread of disorder and suffering. Political leaders can ill afford to ignore these conditions in dense urban communities, where disease and fire can readily spread beyond the boundaries of the slum and ghetto."

What a Satanic prospect!

Where are words to describe the workings of such Socialist teachers' minds? How can fire and disease, disorder and suffering, be of "political advantage" to any group of human beings, no matter who or where they are?

Prof. Cloward and Dr. Piven are indifferent, it seems, to any theory or appeal unrelated to their own determination to create major urban crises in our country and thus "force" a federally dictated general redistribution of income through the guaranteed annual income.

"The growing national movement of welfare recipients," declare Cloward-Piven in their argument for rent revolt, "is already revealing the fiscal punch of tactics which upset the long-standing practices by which local welfare systems withold lawful benefits from the poor. In New York City, for example, organizing drives to claim benefits have forced the welfare rolls up by 50 per cent in less than two years and doubled costs. And this has been accomplished by a movement which has scarcely any funds or organizers of its own."

TO "WORSEN TENSIONS" IN CITIES

Prof. Cloward and Dr. Piven call it a movement. Commissioner Goldberg called it a "conspiracy." That is the right name. What else can anyone call the action proposed by Prof. Cloward and Dr. Piven? In the Leftist radical *Viet Report,* summer 1968, they wrote that the Administration might be forced to alter its spending priorities if strategies could be found "which substantially worsen tensions" in the cities. Who else but a conspirator would want to worsen tensions?

Perhaps that is why federal investigators entered the New York welfare scene. On October 16, the *Daily News* reported, "The federal government will begin a full-scale investigation into New York City welfare policies and administration within 10 days to determine why the number of persons on relief and the costs have soared so dramatically in the city. The State Department of Welfare, in announcing the federal probe, said state officials will work with the U.S. Department of Health, Education and Welfare in carrying out the investigation. The 'special review of public assistance caseloads and costs' is expected to take at least five months to complete."

The federal investigative action was prompted by five New York members of Congress who asked the House Ways and Means Committee to look into the welfare situation in New York City, after Nicholas Kisburg, legislative director of the Teamsters Joint Council 16 had issued a critical report asking some sharp questions, such as, "How effective is the Welfare Department in encouraging and assisting potentially employable recipients to become self-supporting?"

Federal investigators could have gone to church to find an answer. At Broadway United Church of Christ, November

1968, they could have observed that all the welfare mothers present at the Cloward-Piven-indoctrinated meeting, including Mrs. Beulah Sanders, were very well dressed and seemed able-bodied enough to struggle physically against the police in illegal demonstrations.

INTERLOCKING WEB OF PLANNERS

Also at the Broadway church, federal investigators might have gained valuable clues about how to untangle the web of relationships among the Citywide Committee, the National Welfare Rights Organization under directorship of Dr. George A. Wiley, the Columbia University School of Social Work, and the Columbia Center on Social Welfare Policy and Law. If federal investigators were to examine the finances and personnel of these groups and institutions, not only New York City but also other cities in our nation might be able to enjoy a relaxation of tensions among the population and a reduction of expenditures for so-called "welfare." Best of all, the able-bodied but uneducated, untrained poor might receive much more help that really helps.

Federal investigators ought to find out who produced the National Welfare Rights Organization leaflet "The Welfare WIP Program" distributed to coordinators and recruits at the meeting in church. The leaflet was designed to obstruct the Work Incentive Program amendments to the 1967 Social Security Act, which Congress enacted in order to help welfare recipients get off relief rolls.

Maliciously turning "WIP" into "whip," the NWRO leaflet bears a cover illustration showing a Negro woman on her knees on the floor, scrubbing brush in hand and pail nearby, with a cat-o'-nine tails whip poised over her.

At the November 6 meeting in the Broadway United Church of Christ, lawyers and law students from the Columbia Center on Social Welfare Policy and Law instructed "coordinators" how to defy Public Law 90-248, the Work Incentive Program, and other laws and regulations.

A student at the Columbia Center, Jonathan Marsh, briefed the coordinators on the need for getting recruits to fill out papers to back up appeals cases for arrested welfare demonstrators, and also to be presented at welfare "fair hearings" concerning recipients' or applicants' rights to benefits, including telephones and so on.

"Just get recruits to phone in their names and addresses to Citywide in the morning," said young Marsh. "We'll take care of the rest. Most of the recruits never will have to show. We'll fill in the stories and turn in the papers."

Defiance of the law, and perversion of it, is in line with the Cloward-Piven strategy. The two Socialist Scholars are against all "reformist" measures to help the poor: vocational-technical education, rehabilitation, aid by private enterprise. They oppose any and all measures except "outright redistribution of income" in a Socialist state.

On October 26, 1967, Michael Clendenin and Donald Singleton of the N.Y. *Daily News* reported in detail on the campaign waged by Beulah Sanders, Prof. Cloward, Hulbert James and Dr. George A. Wiley "to bring the welfare system to its knees, right now."

GUARANTEED INCOME AS A "RIGHT"

The *Daily News* reporters ended their 1967 article with the rhetorical question, "Will destruction of the existing welfare system accomplish Citywide's goal of a guaranteed annual income?"

Citywide's goal is the Cloward-Piven goal. Dr. Richard A. Cloward and his assistant Dr. Frances Fox Piven at Columbia University School of Social Work, together with their radical pupils at the Columbia Center on Social Welfare Policy and Law, are striving for Marxist goals in which the guaranteed annual income is a huge stepping-stone towards success.

The concept of the guaranteed annual income fulfills the Marxian demand for converting productive workers' hard-earned private individual earnings and savings into public "social" property. It would be used to support an army of bureaucrats handing out a dole to millions of idle, non-productive people. Their ever-growing demands would

In Seattle, Washington, 62 year old Henry T. Buechel, University of Washington economics professor, teaches his class as usual 2/13/70. On 2/11/70. when several activist students attempted to disrupt his class and refused to leave, Buechel took off his coat and glasses and with several students who wanted the class to continue, moved toward the demonstrators with the intent to throw them out. The demonstrators left, shouting obscenities. Buechel thanked his class for its support and said that "no one will ever take over my class." UPI bring about enslavement of working people to local, state, and federal tax collectors.

As things stand now in our country — thanks to our competitive, private, free enterprise system which fosters people's individual desire to get ahead and furnishes them with the incentives to do so — the United States of America is a world Mecca for people seeking economic opportunity and willing to work for it. That happy condition is changing rapidly. Our nation is fast becoming a Mecca for people wanting welfare handouts.

FANTASTIC RISE IN WELFARE COSTS

During the period 1966-1968 which, despite the Vietnam War, was one of unprecedented prosperity, working Americans were called on to shoulder a tax burden for welfare budgets increasing at a fantastically high rate, largely owing to the Cloward welfare strategy of getting people *onto* the welfare rolls. Contrary to what most Americans believe or have been told, total Defense Department expenditures rose by only half a billion dollars from 1968 to 1969, while those of the Department of Health, Education and Welfare (HEW) rose by six billion dollars.

In 1965, the year before the Cloward welfare strategy went into operation, the total of local, state and federal welfare expenditures in our country was $77 billion; in 1968, the total was $112 billion; and in 1969 it was $127 billion, or $48 billion *more* than the total Defense Department expenditures, including those for the Vietnam War!

The greatest error made by most Americans in discussing the soaring welfare costs is to believe that by far the greater part of welfare budgets is spent on aid to the needy, that is, to the blind, disabled and aged. The truth is that such aid requires less than half the total welfare budget, and aid to the blind and disabled is merely a very small fraction of welfare costs.

In the document "Public Welfare Programs: Issues, Problems and Proposals" published by the Tax Foundation, Inc., June 1969, the statistics furnished by the U.S. Department of Health, Education and Welfare show conclusively that there is no major financial problem in our nation involving Federal public assistance aid in cash living allowances to the blind, disabled and aged. In the period 1965-1968, the number of blind persons receiving such Federal aid decreased from 95,000 to 81,000 despite the Vietnam War, with a reduction of $11 million in Federal cash payments. In the same period, 1965-1968, the number of aged persons receiving such Federal cash living allowances decreased by 105,000 and the Federal payments in cash living allowances by $208 million. From 1965 to 1968, however, the number of families with dependent children receiving Federal cash living allowances increased by 1,250,000, and Federal payments of that kind increased by $910,000,000!

The nationwide and local ill effects of Socialist Scholar Cloward's welfare strategy became obvious soon after he wrote his article for *The Nation* in May 1966, and followed it up by his speech to the Second Annual Conference of Socialist Scholars in September of that year.

There was an increase in applications for all forms of relief in New York City alone from 53,000 in 1965 to 74,000 in 1967. During the 12 month period following Dr. Cloward's Wednesday night meetings with New York City welfare clients, the city cash disbursement for "special benefits" went up by $28,000,000! In August 1966, there were 572,251 persons on relief in New York City; in August 1967, there were 742,953. Now in 1970 there are more than a million welfare recipients in the city and the welfare budget exceeds a billion dollars.

For Washington, D.C., the monthly welfare bill increased 71 per cent during fiscal 1969-1970.

In 1965, the New York State budget was $3.48 billion; for 1970 it is $7.26 billion of which $4.2 billion is for "local assistance," meaning mostly education and welfare.

In the two-year period June 1965-June 1967 in New York City, special benefits payments to meet welfare clients' Cloward-coached demands increased by 75% for clothing and 103% for furnishings.

On October 25, 1967, the *New York Daily News* carried an article about the Poverty/Rights Action Program entitled

"Group's Goal: Kill Welfare for Guaranteed Pay." Written by Michael Clendenin and Donald Singleton, the article reported:

"The man who originated the welfare rights program, nearly two years ago, is George Alvin Wiley, a tall, soft-spoken organic chemistry professor at Syracuse University.

"Wiley, who interrupted his teaching in 1964 to serve one year as associate national director of the Congress of Racial Equality (CORE), is director of the Poverty/Rights Action Center in Washington (and director of the National Welfare Rights Movement). . . .

" 'There is no substitute for organized political power,' he said. 'That's the only kind of power this system understands.'

"Wiley said the guaranteed annual income is the only way to wipe out poverty in America. . . .

"The man who is described as 'the brains of the whole movement,' however, is not so reticent as Wiley.

"He is Richard A. Cloward, a professor at the Columbia University School of Social Work. . . ."

On November 27, 1967, the *New York Post* carried an article "Our Welfare Crisis" by Bill Burrus, who reported, "A crisis is building up in the city's $900,000,000 a year welfare system," and he went on to say that "Dr. Richard Cloward and Frances Fox Piven are Columbia University sociologists who want to see the welfare system 'brought to its knees' by overwhelming numbers of legitimate demands that would force a change of the existing system into guaranteed incomes."

Professor Cloward's indoctrinated welfare pupils pushed their letter-of-the-loosely-written-welfare laws demands to such an overwhelming extent that New York City and State soon teetered on the edge of bankruptcy. In August 1968, the New York legislature was forced to abolish the "special welfare benefits" provisions in favor of a "flat grant" system of $100 per welfare recipient in special grants.

Two months later, the *New York Times* reported that Dr. Cloward was in a picket line at New York City Social Service Agency headquarters to protest the new flat grant payments system. The picketing was so illegally conducted that 34 students and social workers were arrested. *The Times* reported,

"Dr. Cloward said that many families who automatically will receive $400 to $500 annually under the new [flat grant] system had been entitled to $1,000 or $1,100 worth of special grants under the old system, but often were not aware of this and so did not apply."

There is no way to write welfare laws so carefully that beneficiaries will not misuse them when coached by teachers of destruction whose real purpose is to destroy our American form of government and establish a Socialist America.

LEADERS NOT FULLY IDENTIFIED

In reporting on the destructive activities of Dr. Richard Cloward and his assistant Dr. Frances Fox Piven, none of the New York City newspapers ever mentioned that they are Socialist Scholars. The *New York Daily News* correctly identified Dr. Cloward as "the brains of the whole (national welfare rights) movement," but did not further identify him as a leading member of the Socialist Scholars Conference, the Marxist braintrust that guides the National Welfare Rights Movement as part of the Old and New Left radical new politics movement, commonly known as "The Movement."

As a main part of its destructive program for the abolition of capitalism in our country, The Movement favors the Cloward welfare strategy as a means of forcing America to adopt the guaranteed annual income.

Chapter 6

REDS AND TERRORISTS

...in Ivy-League Hall

EARLY IN FEBRUARY 1967, the New York City office of Students for a Democratic Society announced that the first major SDS regional Radical Education Project conference would take place at Princeton University, February 17-19, and listed the following participants:

Dave Gilbert, Bob Gottlieb and Gerry Tenney of the New School in New York City (formerly New School for Social Research); Professor Alexander Erlich of Columbia University Economics Department; radical journalist Max Gordon; Jim Jacobs, national REP staff; John Cowley of the New School; John Maher, Harvard SDS; Steve Max, formerly SDS field secretary; Greg Calvert, SDS national secretary; Norman Birnbaum of the New School; John Fuerst,* Columbia SDS; Jim Sommers, City College of New York sociologist; Harry Magdoff, New School economist; Rick Wolff of Yale University; Ray Brown of Sarah Lawrence College Department of Economics; Paul Sweezy, editor, *Monthly Review;* Dr. E. J. Nell.

On February 8, 1967, *The Princetonian* carried the following front page center column news report:

"SDS CONFERENCE CALLED
TO PRESENT EDUCATION
PROJECT
by Chuck Kerr and Joe Field

---

*John Fuerst was arrested in Chicago, October 11, 1969, on charges of mob action, aggravated battery, and resisting arrest.

"The Princeton chapter of Students for a Democratic Society will sponsor the world's first Radical Education Project in McCosh 10, February 17, 18 and 19.

" 'REP,' according to an SDS spokesman, 'is the educational arm of SDS.' It was created to formulate radical left-wing thought through periodic conferences and study groups. . . .

"Although the conference has no practical pretensions, it is intended to make SDS policy more coherent in the future. Many important SDS leaders plan to attend the colloquium. ."

Indeed many important leaders in Students for a Democratic Society (SDS) did attend the Radical Education Project (REP) conference in McCosh Hall at Princeton University during the very cold snowy weekend. So did important Communists and fellow travelers in the Old and New Left. In every way the REP conference at Princeton bore witness to the truth of testimony given on Capitol Hill in Washington, D.C. about Students for a Democratic Society by J. Edgar Hoover, director of the Federal Bureau of Investigation: "Communists are actively promoting and participating in the activities of this organization, which is self-described as a group of liberals and radicals."

FREE REIN FOR EXTREMISTS

If ever there was an "extremist" gathering in our country, that was it. Yet despite Mr. Hoover's public warning about SDS and despite the advance publicity in *The Princetonian,* not a single member of the Princeton University top administration was present at the weekend conference, no trustee was there, and no prominent representative of the student body to take open issue with the Leftists who spent the entire weekend defaming the United States of America.

Absent too were those members of the New York City press and radio-TV broadcasting networks who specialize in bitter opposition to "extremism." Somehow one is forced to doubt the sincerity of "liberal" reporters and broadcasters professing to abhor extremism but recognizing its existence only in groups regarded as "rightists."

There were, for example, no little old ladies in tennis shoes at the Princeton University SDS conference. But there were quite a few little old ladies in galoshes or snow boots who have been long-time supporters of the Socialist Workers Party, and of the Socialist League for Industrial Democracy, though the latter organization claims to have disavowed SDS which is an outgrowth of the Student League for Industrial Democracy.

"I've been a supporter of the L.I.D. for longer than I can remember," said gray-haired Katherine Smith of Long Island to some companions in McCosh Hall, and went on to express her enthusiasm for the young radicals in SDS. "We're struggling with the question," she said in an I-wouldn't-hurt-a-fly voice, "of getting in touch with high school seniors."

A much younger woman present was Mrs. Susan A. Schwartz of Trenton, who talked to SDS members during lunch and recess periods about the New Jersey DuBois Clubs and tried to recruit them into the Communist-controlled groups. "The trouble is," she explained to a woman in her sixties, "some of them really would like to join us, but they think it's best not to because they plan to go into big law firms or industries after college and carry on their radical work from inside them. They feel DuBois Club membership might hurt their chances of getting in to where they want to go. They say otherwise they'd be with us." She paused for breath and went on happily, "But we've been successful with a few. We feel the best way to get them in is through a peace group."

A heavyset, middle-aged man named Abe Weisberg was at the Radical Education Project conference in McCosh 10 at Princeton. A worker in the Spring Mobilization Committee, New York City, he was recruiting participants for a demonstration on April 15 at the United Nations and explained, "We're trying to get on the grounds of the U.N. itself."

In conversations among some recruits there was talk of "organizing training groups on how to break through police lines, get past security guards, and get right into the guts of the places we're going to go. This time we're not going to stay outside police lines at the U.N. We're going to break through, get past security guards, and go right in the headquarters and GA buildings. If there's any rough stuff, they'll be to blame and be exposed for the police brutes and fascists they are."

ACTIVE LONG BEFORE VIETNAM

At the 1967 SDS Princeton conference, there were present not only delegates from the Northeast region of our nation but also "hippies" from San Francisco and agitators from Berkeley. One of the latter told the assembly at Princeton during a discussion from the floor, "I spent nine years working in politics at Berkeley." His statement belied the claim that the radicalization of the University of California at Berkeley in 1964 was due to students' objection to the Vietnam War. Nine years prior to 1967, that is, in 1958, the United States was not involved in a war in Vietnam, but the agitator from Berkeley was involved in his revolutionary work.

In the lectures delivered from the dais in McCosh 10 and during the ensuing discussion periods, the language concerning our country and many of its most prominent civic and business leaders was slanderous but clean, in fact, cultivated, eloquent and even erudite. At mealtimes and between formal sessions, however, the tongues of many SDS members and other youthful participants, both male and female, were as filthy as their fingernails, hair and clothes.

Most REP speakers used modern linguistic equivalents for classical Marxist-Leninist terminology. They argued that under the present American economic system, only "imperialists" and "monopoly capitalists" enjoy affluence and adequate consumption; the working class majority, they claimed, suffers from "scarcity" and any "post-scarcity" economy would therefore have to be a Socialist one.

A Columbia University student, who said that the American people enjoy the highest living standard and widest mass consumption of goods and services in the world, seemed to be somewhat shaken by the proceedings at McCosh. He asked a few penetrating questions during open discussion from the floor. Later another Columbia student, evidently troubled, cornered Dave Gilbert during lunch hour and pressed him for a statement of SDS-REP aims.

"Eventually," said Gilbert, "we seek to create a Communist society in which everything will be decentralized and there will be no formal educational institutions. People wanting to know things will seek out persons with knowledge."

The Columbia student asked how SDS intends to achieve radical change in American society.

"We use the technique of demands," explained Gilbert, "always pushing and pushing on through demands, to an end where they have to give in or fight against the revolution."

DEPICT U.S. AS "MONSTER"

On Saturday afternoon, Greg Calvert, newly elected National Secretary of Students for a Democratic Society, addressed the Princeton conference. Clean-shaven except for a small brush mustache, and wearing his light brown hair just a little long at the back, Calvert jokingly described himself as a "prairie dog" visitor to the East from the Prairie State and began his speech with the declaration, "The movement for radical change in America is going through change." He said radicals must now "orient themselves toward the third world revolution." It is against, he said, "the American monster." Defining the monster as "American corporate capitalism," he characterized it as "incredibly brutal at home and abroad." He described the new radicalism in America as coming from "deep gut level perception of human beings" and defined this perception as "revolutionary class consciousness—to use traditional vocabulary."

The main aim of the SDS-Rep conference at Princeton during the mid-February weekend was to depict the United States of America as a monster.

When white-haired Paul Sweezy, editor of the Far Leftist *Monthly Review*, was introduced to the SDS gathering, all were urged to buy his book *Monopoly Capital*, written with the late Paul A. Baran, and described as "must" reading. Copies were on sale outside McCosh 10 throughout the week-end. Published in 1966, the book bears the dedication "For Ché" —probably meaning guerrilla fighter Ché Guevara of Red Cuba—and the following quotation on a flyleaf:

"Two centuries ago, a former European colony decided to catch up with Europe. It succeeded so well that the United States of America became a monster in which the taints, the sickness, and the inhumanity of Europe have grown to appalling dimensions.

—Frantz Fanon"

Sweezy writes in a preface to his book, "One type of criticism we would like to answer in advance. We shall probably be accused of exaggerating. It is a charge to which we readily plead guilty. In a very real sense the function of both science and art is to exaggerate, provided that what is exaggerated is truth and not falsehood."

Sweezy's sophistry is characteristic of his tortured Marxist dialectic, for truth is truth and, being so, cannot be exaggerated. From the dais in McCosh 10, Sweezy said the technology of 20th century capitalism is merely "perfected means of destruction" and tied solely to profits. "It follows," he said, "you cannot reform this monopoly capitalist system—all the welfare state does is merely emasculate opposition to the system." Didactically, Sweezy announced, "The only hope is to overthrow the system."

Again and again, Sweezy and the REP conference leaders urged the participants to study *Monopoly Capital*, which ends with the mad Hitler-Stalin type statement, "The drama of our time is the world revolution; it can never come to an end until it has encompassed the whole world."

THE BASIC CONCEPT OF LENIN

Earlier that day, on Sunday morning at McCosh, a Red sermon was delivered to the SDS-REP conference by "Professor" Harry Magdoff of the New School in New York City. He discussed his paper "The Economics of U.S.

Imperialism" (published by *Monthly Review* press, 1966) and portrayed our country as a military-industrial monster seeking "to colonize" Western Europe through corporate foreign investments. He showed several charts on a large teaching screen to prove that the domestic internal U.S. economy during the last ten years has been stagnating except for sales and profits derived from exploitation of foreign markets and from military expansion. Having branded the U.S. oil industry with the single sweeping Marxist generalization "oil is pure imperialism of the most arrogant sort," Magdoff turned the heat of his radical ire on General Motors and General Electric, especially the latter.

"I very deliberately didn't prepare a paper," he began his speech, in a palsy-walsy way, smiling at the young people. "All of you read the paper I gave at the Socialist Scholars Conference." Then he praised "the very fruitful discussions I had last weekend at Ithaca with the SDS group."

At this time of writing in 1970, there has not been any investigation, to the best of my knowledge, of Harry Magdoff's activities with SDS members at Cornell University, a place that suffered from a terrible outbreak of armed violence in 1969, an outbreak from which that university has not recovered, and which caused several accomplished and outstanding professors to resign from the faculty in protest at the weak policies followed by the administration at Cornell.

Evidently Harry Magdoff gets around today with the same nimbleness as in the past. But he is not nearly so reluctant to speak out now as he has been on certain momentous occasions. At Princeton University among fellow radicals, he was willing to state his real intellectual and political position. "All this," he told the SDS-REP conference about the notes, charts and remarks he was presenting, "is within a certain logic, the basic concept of Lenin. My argument supports that."

He has supported it for a long time, even during his employment in the U.S. Government from New Deal days until 1946.

On May 1, 1953, Harry Magdoff was questioned by the Senate Internal Security Subcommittee and took the Fifth

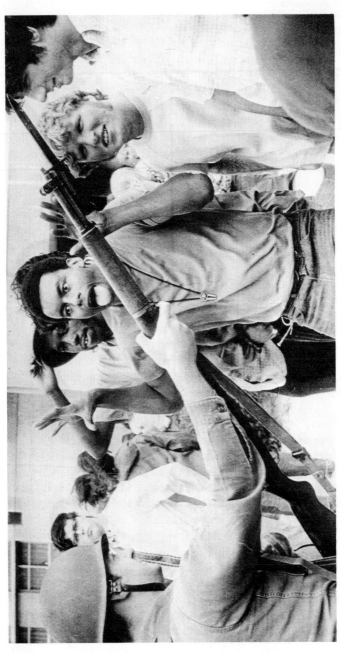

A young student protestor gives an Illinois National Guardsman a rough time after the Guard moved on the Southern Illinois University campus (Carbondale, Ill.) to enforce a 7:30 p.m. curfew, 5/8/70. Mayor David Keene declared a state of civil emergency after a night of violence and vandalism on 5/7/70. UPI

Amendment in reply to the question whether he was "at this very moment a member of a secret and espionage ring" operating against the interests of the U.S. Government by Communists and on behalf of the Soviet Union.

With such a record, known for so long, it seems inconceivable that Harry Magdoff should be on the faculty of even such a left-of-center institution as the New School, and almost incredible that he should be permitted to occupy the dais in McCosh 10 at Princeton University to defame our country, its industrial corporations, economic and social system, and political leaders without there having been present to challenge him anyone from the Princeton Administration, or board of trustees, or student government. Granted that most of the young people in McCosh 10 were well aware of and in sympathy with Magdoff's Marxist-Leninist views, there seemed to be present a few young men and women who, like the uneasy, questioning Columbia student, were troubled at what they heard. Had its objectivity been effectively disputed by a Princeton University faculty member or respected Princeton official, perhaps the uncertain young people might have been enlightened and would have quit the conference.

NACLA ATTACKS U.S. IN LATIN AMERICA

An undeluded young person there, however, was a beautiful pint-sized blonde dressed in pale lavender and looking as innocent as the driven snow on the campus outside the Chapel across from McCosh Hall. Though not listed as a speaker on the official SDS-REP program, she mounted the dais on Sunday morning to deliver a paper harshly critical of American enterprise in Latin America and especially in Brazil.

What U.S. investment in Latin America does, she charged, is to set up "foreign enclaves" in the underdeveloped Latin economies. She quoted but twisted the meaning of a statement by George Moore, then president of the First National City Bank of New York, to prove her point, and pronounced his name as if it were that of the devil himself.

It was astonishing to hear the little blonde speak so coldly about economics for she was introduced as "Edith Black of Union Theological Seminary," and she looks like an angel with pink-and-white complexion and long flowing wavy golden hair.

"I am a revolutionist," she told an elderly woman during lunch hour. "Not just a Marxist, a revolutionist." Miss Black discussed with a few friends—all very much in the inside SDS—her contacts with friends at the Leftist radical *Ramparts Magazine*. "We're working on quite a few situations," she said, and added with a sweet smile, "They'll rock the nation."

When she said "We're doing research on it," the average American would think she meant that she and her friends are doing research on what makes the flowers bloom in May and snowflakes dance in December. But what she really means by "research" was made clear to the REP conference participants while she was on the dais and with charming feminine deference paid highest intellectual tribute to Harry Magdoff.

It seems Miss Edith Black is a very hard worker. She not only attended classes at Union Theological Seminary but also worked in a cubicle on the 9th floor at 475 Riverside Drive with a group called "NACLA," North American Congress on Latin America. There was talk at the SDS-REP conference at Princeton of creating a new NACLA magazine to "blow" revelations about the CIA and "bring down" the "reactionary" governments of several Latin American countries.

At that time, almost no one in our country ever had heard of NACLA, and that was the first time I myself had heard of it. Worried over the way young Edie Black and the SDS members talked about NACLA, including several young women whose names I didn't get but whose hate-filled faces became etched in my memory, I formed the opinion that the North American Congress on Latin America (NACLA) had dangerously harmful potentialities and later said so in a newspaper column and in an article for *U.S.A. Magazine* that was reprinted on the front page of *Barron's*.

TERRORIST AT PRINCETON

A year and nine months later, on November 14, 1969, I picked up the morning newspapers to read at breakfast and saw huge front page headlines announcing that three men and a woman had been arrested in New York City and charged with being "left-radical terrorists who had set off the bombs in eight major corporate and governmental structures in the city since July."

A fifth suspect—said the papers—was being sought in the alleged conspiracy.

Interrupted by a phone call, after breakfast, I didn't finish reading the story. That evening I turned on the six o'clock television news, heard and saw all about the arrested suspects, four of whom later pleaded guilty, and was watching the TV screen intently when suddenly I was startled to recognize the face of a young woman, the fifth bombing suspect, who, explained the newscaster, was being sought in connection with the bombings.

"Good heavens!" I cried aloud, recognizing her as one of the young women who had been at the SDS Radical Education Project conference at Princeton University in February 1967.

Her name, I learned in the newscast, is Pat Swinton. At this time of writing, she is wanted by the F.B.I. as a fugitive from justice.

When the news broadcast was ended, that November 1969 evening, I hurriedly got my copy of that day's *New York Times* and read the whole long story of the sensational arrests by the F.B.I., including the following account in *The Times*:

"Being sought is 22-year-old Pat Swinton, who also lived at the East Fourth Street address and who formerly worked in an organization called the North American Congress on Latin America, which the F.B.I. said 'correlates research' on what the group calls 'U.S. imperialism in Latin America' ".

The *New York Times* further reported that along with George Demmerle, Jane Lauren Alpert, John D. Hughey 3rd and Samuel Joseph Melville, the Swinton girl is accused of setting off or planting bombs during 1969 at the following times and places:

July 27 — A United Fruit Company Pier on the Hudson River;

Aug. 20 — Marine Midland Grace Trust Company Building at 26 Federal Plaza;

Oct. 7 — United States Armed Forces Examining and Entrance Station, 39 Whitehall Street;

Nov.11 — RCA Building at Rockefeller Plaza; General Motors Building at Fifth Avenue and 59th Street, and the Chase Manhattan Building, 1 Chase Manhattan Plaza;

Nov.12 — Criminal Courts Building, 100 Centre Street, and an Army truck parked near the 68th Regimental Armory at 26th St. and Lexington Ave.

In the bombing of the Marine Midland Grace Trust Building, a bomb equal in force to 24 sticks of dynamite exploded, injuring 19 night workers at the bank. Fifty people were working there at the time and it was a miracle they were not killed or gravely hurt.

On the night of November 14, 1969, I stayed up to listen to the eleven o'clock news and to see again the face of the vanished Pat Swinton on screen. Afterwards I went to my files and took out a copy of my 1967 article on the SDS Radical Education Project conference at Princeton University.

It made me sick to read my own reporting—sick at heart and in spirit, because I had tried so hard with so little result, apparently, to warn the public in general, and academic community in particular, about the coming disastrous consequences to our country in their pursuing a policy of permissiveness with the revolutionary communist Students for a Democratic Society and other Leftist radical groups all closely affiliated with the Socialist Scholars.

During that winter weekend in February 1967, the worst element among "The Movement" accomplished exactly what they wanted in McCosh Hall at Princeton. They entered a citadel of traditional American society and could thereafter use Princeton's prestige in their effort to overthrow our society.

Classes for thousands of students were cancelled 5/5/70 in a partially effective strike at the University of California in Berkeley. Hundreds of anti-war demonstrators roamed the campus battling with police. A bearded demonstrator hurls back a tear gas canister at police.   UPI

As the conference broke up at Princeton, late Sunday afternoon, a hard-working campus maintenance personnel man watched the departing participants, most of them dirty and unkempt, and said in disgust, "This weekend this university needed two things: a Joe McCarthy and this year's football team to scrimmage those characters out of the place."

Chapter 7

"NEW POLITICS"

...Led By Revolutionaries

ON APRIL 15, 1967, a huge demonstration for "peace" took place at United Nations Plaza in New York City. It was led by the New Politics coalition of Leftists and Communists, all working together in two nationwide propaganda campaigns named "Spring Mobilization" and "Vietnam Summer."

During that demonstration, William S. Pepper, then a faculty member at Mercy College in Westchester County, N.Y., who had become executive director of the National Conference for New Politics (NCNP), declared over the public address system:

"What is needed to begin to restore our humanity is *revolution!* For the Federal agents in attendance, what I mean is not violent overthrow of the United States Government but development of a revolutionary force which will combine nationally, for the first time, the energy and idealism of The Movement with radical political sophistication, a combination in which radical political change can also naturally flow from, among other tactics, the effective use of civil disobedience."

While hundreds of police were guarding U.N. Headquarters from invasion by the demonstrators, a meeting was taking place inside the U.N. Church Center of a private organization called the United States Committee for the Christian Peace Conference. This is a Marxist group who allegedly were trying to promote a dialogue between Christian clergymen in the West and "Christian" Marxists in Socialist nations behind the Iron Curtain.

A main speaker at that meeting was Dr. Robert Cohen, a member of the Socialist Scholars, chairman of the Boston University physics department and chairman of the American Institute for Marxist Studies, the main educational and propaganda arm of the Communist Party, U.S.A.

SOME PEACE CORPS VETERANS INVOLVED

It was there that I first learned about the existence of a movement to recruit returned Peace Corps workers into a Committee of Returned Volunteers (CRV) to use their special knowledge of foreign lands, gained at American taxpayers' expense, for promotion of revolution at home and abroad. Director J. Edgar Hoover of the F.B.I. testified before a Subcommittee of the House Committee on Appropriations, March 5, 1970, that the Committee of Returned Volunteers, numbering approximately 1,000 members in a dozen cities, had held a national assembly in rural Minnesota, September 1969, during which the CRV called for a "new society" with goals that could not be achieved "unless there is a revolution in the Third World [meaning in the free nations of Asia, Africa and Latin America] and in the United States."

At the April 1967 U.N. Church Center meeting, Alice Hageman, head of the Peace Service of the Young Generation, Christian Peace Conference, said she was helping to organize the Committee of Returned Volunteers.

Recruiters for it were working out of the office of Professor Immanuel Wallerstein, in the sociology department at Columbia University, and they were collaborating with members of the University Christian Movement, with the SDS Radical Education Project, and with the North American Congress on Latin America. Members of all these groups held secret meetings at night in Earl Hall at Columbia.

330 LEFTIST GROUPS COLLABORATE

At McMillin Theater, August 17, 1967, that university also was the site of a very important meeting of the New York chapter of the National Conference for New Politics prior to that organization's nationwide convention over Labor Day weekend at the Palmer House in Chicago.

Among the active supporters of the NCNP convention were Arnold Johnson (New York), Dorothy Healey (California) and Claude Lightfoot (Illinois) of the Communist Party, U.S.A. The NCNP convention in Chicago ended in raucous dispute between Black Power and white militants, a dispute that hit nationwide headlines. The conferees did $14,000 damage to the Palmer House.

Thereafter the National Conference for New Politics went out of existence as a single, all-embracing bureaucratic organization. But the loose association of more than 330 Leftist organizations which took part in the Chicago NCNP convention continued to work closely together under the generic term "New Politics" and the slogan "1968 And Beyond."

They worked together so effectively, and were able to create such a great degree of dissension among Americans, that President Lyndon B. Johnson announced, March 31, 1968, he would not be a candidate in the forthcoming presidential election.

Immediately, the New Politics leaders boasted they had forced him "to abdicate." Then they moved forward with a plan to disrupt the 1968 Democratic National Convention in Chicago and force nomination by the Democratic Party of a presidential candidate favoring New Politics.

Though the New Politics leaders did not succeed in controlling the convention, they did succeed in creating a violent situation in the streets that rocked the nation and shook its very foundations. Every important aspect of that violence was the direct result of planning by the revolutionary New Politics groups. All the planning was done by radical Leftists.

REAL LEADERS NOT EXPOSED

Stunned with horrified amazement at the sight on the television screen of the hateful violence in Chicago, millions upon millions of Americans, regardless of party affiliation,

In Washington, D.C., a plainclothes officer dodges a chunk of ice being thrown by a protester during a demonstration 2/19/70 protesting the convictions in the Chicago riot conspiracy trial. The officer, along with a second policeman (dark glasses, right) were arresting another demonstrator at George Washington University where the incident occurred. The demonstrators had marched to the Watergate apartment complex where Attorney General Mitchell makes his home, but returned to the school area after a confrontation with police.   UPI demanded to know why and how such a dreadful thing could have happened. They were given every kind of off-the-cuff, emotional and self-serving answer. They also were furnished with allegedly impartial but Left-biased interim reports written under contract to the National Commission on the Causes and Prevention of Violence, which had been created on June 10, 1968, five days after the assassination of Senator Robert F. Kennedy in Los Angeles.

What the American people did not receive was solid information on which to base a well-informed opinion concerning the ever growing violence in our communities. We never were furnished with a clear account of the New Politics movement, though it was and is ideologically responsible for the violence and is led by Socialist professors and their Marxist associates.

Though the record of their leading role in intimate collaboration is a matter of historical fact, they are not identified for what they really are in the interim reports issued by the Commission on the Causes and Prevention of Violence appointed by President Johnson, or in testimony before President Nixon's Commission on Campus Unrest.

THE IDENTIFICATION GAP

It is this lack of identification, in my judgment, that leads to most of the confusion concerning who really is who, and what really is what, in the tragic series of violent events in our nation since the assassination of President John F. Kennedy in November 1963 by Lee Harvey Oswald, a Marxist revolutionary, who cried out after his arrest, "I want Abt!", meaning John Abt, long-time lawyer for the Communist Party, U.S.A.

There has been a vast amount of talk about alleged or real gaps in our society — missile and credibility gaps, for example. In my opinion, the most extensive gap is an Identification Gap. It is creating an unnecessary crisis of confusion and dissension among us, a crisis largely due to lack of accurate information about the real political bias of our internal enemies. No fair-minded person would tolerate baseless or bigoted charges against any human being. But it is imperative in our revolutionary times, haunted by the threat of totalitarianism, for a free people to know the real political and ideological views of persons seeking to overthrow our form of government and to control us as a people.

No single example of the identification gap is more striking or typical than the omission of any reference to the identity of the person who assassinated President Kennedy in the book *A Thousand Days—John F. Kennedy in the White House* by Pulitzer prize historian Arthur M. Schlesinger Jr., who is a professor at the City University of New York, and was a close adviser to President Kennedy and a founder of Americans for Democratic Action. The book does not contain the name of assassin Lee Harvey Oswald in the text or index, much less the politically significant fact that he was a Marxist revolutionary and member of the pro-Communist Fair Play for Cuba Committee. Thus an uninformed student or citizen wanting to learn the history of the thousand days during which President Kennedy was in office can be tricked into ignorance of the fact that there was such a person as Lee Harvey Oswald and of the terrible role he played.

Similarly, an uninformed person reading "The Politics of Protest—Violent Aspects of Protest & Confrontation," an interim report to the National Commission on The Causes and Prevention of Violence prepared by Dr. Jerome H. Skolnick, of the University of California at Berkeley, and by his fellow researchers at its Center for the Study of Law and Society, omits vitally important information.

The Skolnick Report states that four university professors were the intellectuals mainly responsible for organizing the New Politics protest movement in 1965—Staughton Lynd, then of Yale University, Noam Chomsky of Massachusetts Institute of Technology, Franz Schurmann of the University of California at San Diego, and Howard Zinn of Boston University. Yet the report describes the four merely as influential professors, not as the dedicated Marxists they really are.

Either Dr. Skolnick omitted factual identification of the four for fear of a charge of "McCarthyism," or he deliberately chose not to identify them as Marxist-biased intellectuals.

Yet American taxpayers who paid for the interim Skolnick Report have a right to receive the specific information they paid for.

Here is the Skolnick Report reference (page 42) to the four academic ringleaders of a movement which claims to be grounded on objection to U.S. Government policy in Vietnam but actually is based on Marxist antipathy for anti-Communist effort made by our traditional American society:

". . . The [Vietnam protest] movement itself consisted largely of people who *do* pay attention to intellectuals, and the movement conceived its first task to be a scholarly one: to expose the contradictions and half-truths in the standard government account of the war. The absence of widely respected left-of-center political spokesmen made for a vacuum into which the intellectuals were drawn. Professors like Noam Chomsky, Staughton Lynd, Franz Schurmann and Howard Zinn not only disseminated information but also helped define the movement's consciousness, as, for example, in Professor Chomsky's influential essay 'The Responsibility of the Intellectuals' ".

Not a single word in the Skolnick Report reveals that Staughton Lynd, formerly of Yale, and Franz Schurmann, of the University of California at Berkeley, are members of the Socialist Scholars. Not a single word in the Skolnick Report reveals that Staughton Lynd and Howard Zinn were original advisers to Students for a Democratic Society in creating their Radical Education Project at Ann Arbor, Michigan. Still worse, not one of the four Marxist intellectuals—Lynd, Chomsky, Schurmann and Zinn—was summoned as a witness during the three days of hearings conducted by Dr. Skolnick's task force on "Violent Aspects of Protest and Confrontation."

Yet each of the four played a major role in the destructive New Politics movement that fomented the protests and violent confrontations. As far as their exposure of contradictions and half-truths in the U.S. Government account of the Vietnam War is concerned, the Skolnick Report does not inform readers that Marxists are doctrine-bound to "expose the contradictions" in any non-Communist endeavor during peace or war.

SOURCE OF FUNDS

Though the manifestations of the New Politics movement appear in communities throughout the nation, the main think-tank operations were set up by four groups. These are:

(1) The Center for the Study of Democratic Institutions at Santa Barbara, California, which is subsidized mainly by the Fund for the Republic;

(2) the Institute for Policy Studies in Washington, D.C., which is subsidized by several private individuals and foundations, including the Ford, Milbank, Field, Cudahy, and Samuel Rubin foundations, the Edgar Stern Family Fund, and the Fontaney Corporation through James P. Warburg;

(3) the Students for a Democratic Society Radical Education Project, which is subsidized by New Politics leftists and possibly by funds channeled from Havana, Hanoi, Prague, Peiping and Moscow; and

(4) the Socialist Scholars Conference organization, which was originally subsidized mainly by the Louis M. Rabinowitz Foundation.

A brief outline of New Politics history was recited to members of the New York chapter of the National Conference for New Politics in August 1967 at Columbia University by William S. Pepper, executive director of NCNP. He said it was "the brainchild of a small group of academicians and theorists who met on the West Coast in the summer of 1965."

They met at the Center for the Study of Democratic Institutions at Santa Barbara, and Pepper told the absolute truth. It absolutely belies the prevailing myth in our country that the radical protests on our campuses and in our communities are the product of spontaneous outbreaks by students and by people living in city slum areas or backward rural regions.

The small group of academicians and theorists to whom William Pepper referred included Julian Bond, Simon Casady

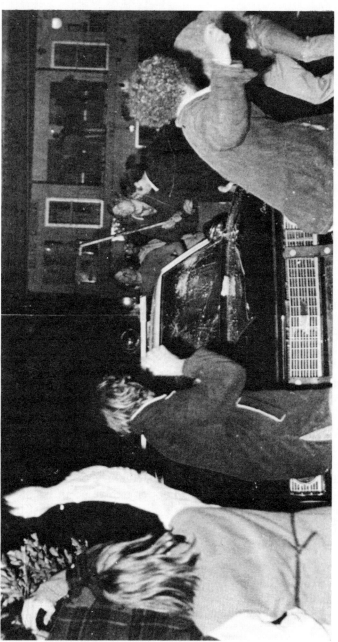

Demonstrators, in Santa Barbara, California, protesting the "Chicago Seven" riot trial, pelt a police car before setting it afire. Some 1,000 demonstrators, many from the University of California later went on a rampage in the Isla Vista section of the city smashing windows, starting fires and pelting police with rocks, 2/25/70.   UPI and Stokely Carmichael, among many others, and the first document the group issued, "A Call To A New Politics," was signed by Farrel Broslawsky; John Buchanan; Simon Casady (ousted from the leftist California Democratic Council for his extremism); Philip Drath; W. H. Ferry (formerly vice president of the Center for the Study of Democratic Institutions); Josh Gould; Daniel Grey; John Haag; Michael Hannon; Hallock Hoffman (formerly secretary-treasurer of the Center at Santa Barbara, now chairman of the leftist Pacifica Foundation); Richard Miller; Robert Scheer (then publisher of *Ramparts* magazine); Stanley Scheinbaum (staff member of the Center at Santa Barbara); and Harvey Wheeler (also a staff member at the Center).

The introduction to the first "Call to New Politics"states:

"One of the things that is 'new' about the New Politics is that it dedicates itself to remaining permanently radical."

The first page of the "Call" refers to "the evils surrounding all aspects of life in America." As defined in the Call, New Politics is "pressure point politics . . . operating directly on society's most vulnerable points." The Call also described New Politics as "guerrilla politics" and "liberation front politics" and "revolutionary politics." The Call declared that the evils accompanying the process of capital formation "can be exterminated at their roots." The Call called for total regulation and control of business "by the states and cities."

Soon after issuance of the first "Call to New Politics" there came a second Call written by Arthur I. Waskow of the Institute for Policy Studies. Thereafter a great many New Politics activities — as William Pepper explained in his short history of the movement — were transferred to that institute in our nation's capital.

IDENTITY OF LEADERS

The Waskow Call formed almost the entire text of the final formal "Call to Convention" issued by the National Conference for New Politics in 1967, and that formal Call was signed by all members of the NCNP Steering Committee, who were:

Michael P. Wood, Chairman

Julian Bond
    Georgia House of Represen-
    tatives

Paul Booth
    Executive Board, NCNP

Chet Briggs
    Texas Center for New Politics

William Clay*
    Alderman, St. Louis

Ivanhoe Donaldson
    Student Nonviolent Coordi-
    nating Committee

David Frost
    New Jersey Political Alliance

Bertram Garskof
    Ann Arbor Citizens for New
    Politics

Carlton Goodlett
    California Democratic Council

Victoria Gray
    Mississippi Freedom Demo-
    cratic Party

Jerome Grossman
    Massachusetts Political Action
    for Peace

Richard Hatcher[†]
    Councilman, Gary, Ind.

Myles Horton
    Highlander Center

John Hulett
    Lowndes County Freedom
    Organization

Thomas Nerney
    American Independent Move-
    ment, Conn.

A.A. Rayner
    Alderman, Chicago

Mrs. Kenneth Montgomery*[†]
    Executive Board, NCNP

Robert Scheer
    Berkeley Community for New
    Politics

Stanley Sheinbaum
    Santa Barbara Community for
    New Politics

Benjamin Spock, M.D.
    Executive Board, NCNP

Susan Thrasher
    Executive Board, NCNP

Lawrence Victor
    Minnesota Peace Cooperative

Robert Washburn
    Society for New Action Poli-
    tics, Portland

Arthur Waskow
    Institute for Policy Studies

Andrew J. Young
    Southern Christian Leadership
    Conference

---

*Later elected to U.S. House of Representatives.

†Later elected Mayor, Gary, Indiana.

*†Mrs. Kenneth Montgomery (Lucy Montgomery) wealthy Chicago subsidizer
of the National Conference for New Politics and other radical groups.

The members of the New Politics executive board were: *

Paul Albert
Donna Allen
Julian Bond
Paul Booth
Stokely Carmichael
Simon Casady
Rev. William Sloane Coffin, Jr.
Victoria Gray
Dick Gregory
Miss Terry Jefferson
Mrs. Kenneth Montgomery
Martin Peretz

Don Rothenberg
Robert Scheer
Benjamin Spock, M.D.
Marc Stone
Susan Thrasher
Monroe Wasch
Arthur I. Waskow
Lee Webb
Peter Weiss
Henry J. Wineberg
Michael Wood

The members of the National Conference for New Politics national council, with Julian Bond and Simon Casady as co-chairmen, were: *

Paul Albert
Donna Allen
Josiah Beeman
Julian Bond
Paul Booth
Samuel Bowles
Robert Browne
Jane Buchenholz
Stokely Carmichael
Simon Casady
Rev. William Sloane Coffin, Jr.
Mrs. Gardner Cox
June Oppen Degnan
Ronnie Dugger
W.H. Ferry
Erick Fromm
Edward P. Gottlieb
Victoria Gray
Dick Gregory
Jerome Grossman

Alfred Hassler
Nat Hentoff
Warren Hinckle
Hallock Hoffmann
H. Stuart Hughes
Miss Terry Jefferson
Byron L. Johnson
Rev. Martin Luther King, Jr.
Irving F. Laucks
Sidney Lens
Herbert Marcuse
Lenore Marshall
Frances McAllister
Carey McWilliams
Stewart Meacham
Seymour Melman
Everett Mendelsohn
Mrs. Kenneth Montgomery
Paul O'Dwyer
Martin Peretz

*The original document does not identify the persons. Some are well-known. They are all listed so that readers may identify professors, teachers and other personalities known in their communities or institutions.

Gifford Phillips	William Strickland
Thomas Francis Ritt	Albert Szent-Gyorgyi, M.D.
Sumner Rosen	Harold Taylor
Don Rothenberg	Susan Thrasher
Richard A. Russell	Michael Walzer
Marshall Sahlins	Monroe Wasch
Robert Scheer	Arthur I. Waskow
Michael Schneider	Lee Webb
Robert Schwartz	Peter Weiss
Benjamin Spock, M.D.	Henry J. Wineberg
Marc Stone	Michael Wood

The Waskow Call to New Politics ended with the exhortation "Don't mourn for America — ORGANIZE!"

THEY ORGANIZE FOR VIOLENCE

That is exactly what the Leftist radicals in The Movement did during the remainder of 1967, and continually in 1968 until the Democratic National Convention and thereafter. The united Leftist front in our country, known as The Movement and working in New Politics, organized from one end of the nation to the other under the slogan "1968 And Beyond." They organized for ten days of violence in campus rebellions in April 1968; they organized for the terrible events that took place at Harvard, Cornell, San Francisco State and the Universities of Michigan, Minnesota, Wisconsin, Southern California and many others in 1969, and for worse events at Kent State University, Ohio State University and Jackson State College in Mississippi in 1970.

Relentlessly, they organized and moved on, step by step, and always under the intellectual guidance of professors belonging to the Socialist Scholars and their Marxist associates acting as members of a national and international network of revolutionaries.

At Columbia University, August 17, 1967, William S. Pepper stressed the dual intellectual and political nature of New Politics and said flatly, "The press doesn't understand it."

In a sense he was dead right.

Many editorial policy makers in the big communications media didn't and don't understand it. A few leading policy makers do understand it, but are unwilling to explain it objectively because they themselves are in sympathy with it. By "it" I mean the dual intellectual and political nature of New Politics in which revolutionary advocacy and action are two like parts.

Chapter 8

SUBSIDIZED SUBVERSION

...Riots and Bombings

THOUGH THE PRESS reported on the factional break-up of the National Conference for New Politics at its 1967 Labor Day convention in Chicago as if that were the end of that, almost all of the principals and several hundred participants from all states in our union had merely adjourned, since they reassembled the following weekend at the Third Annual Conference of Socialist Scholars in the New York Hilton Hotel.

A very large audience attended the opening Saturday afternoon discussion on "Poverty in America" at which Michael Harrington was the star speaker. He is chairman of the Socialist League for Industrial Democracy and wrote *The Other America*, a book that was published in 1961 and inspired the Kennedy Administration's poverty program.

Right off the bat, Mr. Harrington told the Socialist gathering that he had told Sargent Shriver, head of the Office of Economic Opportunity (OEO) in the Kennedy Administration, "You are offering only crumbs to the poor."

Yet for fiscal 1967, Congress had appropriated $1.87 billion for the OEO, which "crumbs" amount to a third of the average annual total U.S. Government expenditures for *all* purposes during the Roosevelt New Deal period 1931-1935.

For fiscal 1968, Congress appropriated the sums of $40.7 billion for Health, Education and Welfare (HEW) and $1.9 billion for Housing and Urban Development. Thus for fiscal

1968, the total amount appropriated by Congress for Federal aid to citizens was $42.6 billion, exclusive of $7.79 billion for aid to veterans.

These "crumbs" were a load on American taxpayers that amounted to one-eighth the total 1967 gross national product of the 176,000,000 people living and working in the Common Market countries of Western Europe, that is, France, West Germany, Italy, Belgium, Luxembourg and The Netherlands.

"We ourselves have to make a revolution for the entire society," Michael Harrington told his fellow Socialists.

REVOLUTION RATHER THAN REFORM

His speech was followed by harangues from Hyman Lumer, national education secretary of the Communist Party, U.S.A., and from Stanley Aronowitz, then chairman of a New Politics group in Manhattan. Both speakers argued for radicalism rather than reformism in pushing our country along the path to revolution.

Stanley Aronowitz tore into Harrington's thesis of peaceful democratic socialist reform, identified himself with "a revolutionary action group," and said only such a group could attain Socialist objectives in America.

"Okay, if you think it will work, I'm all for it," said Harrington, ceding under pressure from the Communists, as is almost always the case when soft socialists come under direct fire from hard ones.

Two years later, when radicals had grown much bolder in our country, Aronowitz told a Socialist Scholars meeting in Town Hall, Manhattan, the specific nature of his action. "We cannot permit any of the radical movement to be clamped down by the government," he said. "We, as revolutionary Communists, must defend all those taking part in revolutionary action. . ."

In 1967, at the Hilton Hotel meeting, Aronowitz called for destruction of the existing power structure and authority in our country. "Racism is based on the profit system," he declared.

The police, claimed Aronowitz, are the arm of the ruling class in the ghettoes. "They are the oppressors," he said.

Violently, Aronowitz attacked the entire Poverty Program except for a single aspect which he described as "a valuable tool" for the radical movement. "At least," he said, "it has given employment to the organizers."

The audience burst into laughter, applause and cheers. "That's right, man," called out someone from the floor. "It gave our organizers some bread."

In New Left slang, "bread" means "money."

INSTANCES OF SUBSIDIZED SUBVERSION

Thus, out of their own mouths, Communists among the Socialist Scholars confirmed charges made by *Barron's National Business and Financial Weekly,* July 31, 1967, in an article headed "Poverty Warriors — The Riots Are Subsidized As Well As Organized." The weekly publication stated, "From the beginning, as radicals recognized, the war on poverty, notably the Community Action Programs, had impressive trouble-making potentials." Quoting its Washington correspondent, Shirley Scheibla, *Barron's* cited specific cases of poverty-program-subsidized subversion, for example: John Ross, member of the Maoist Progressive Labor Party, served on an anti-poverty board in San Francisco; Howard Harawitz, former member of the W.E.B. DuBois Clubs, served on a similar board in Berkeley; John Zippert, participant in the Moscow-financed World Youth Festival, and Shirley Mesher, member of the Marxist-Leninist Black Panther Party, served together in an OEO-financed project in Selma, Alabama. *Barron's* cited reports of similar taxpayer-financed poverty program subversion in Washington, D.C., Cleveland, Newark, Perth Amboy, N.J., Rochester, N.Y., and other riot-torn communities.

BLACK POWER AIMS

While comfortable, complacent Americans went to church or played golf or lolled around at home reading the papers or watching television, Sunday morning, September 10, a Black Power panel session took place at the Socialist Scholars Conference. The chairman was James Boggs of Detroit; the panelists were Raymond S. Franklin of Queens College, N.Y., Ivanhoe Donaldson, campaign manager for Julian Bond in Georgia and a member of the Student Non-Violent Co-ordinating Committee ("Snick") and Gilbert Osofky of the University of Illinois, Chicago.

It is too bad that other reporters besides myself, and some Congressional investigators were not present. They would have found out the frightening facts of life in our nation today. They would have heard Chairman Boggs say no Socialist can deny the validity of the classic Leninist concept of the inevitability of conflict between capitalist and socialist society, and that in America today, "There is a growth of a force inside the society that makes conflict and violence inevitable," and Ivanhoe Donaldson say "The tentacles of the American octopus reach out into 55 areas of the world to-day, and our problem is destroying the eye of the octopus here at home."

James Boggs declared, "Black Power is a scientific concept whose time has come." He described it as "clashing with every segment of society," and said it must "bring the struggle to the streets." He said, "Black Power raises the concrete question of the taking of power, of mobilizing one set of people to replace another set of people."

Chairman Boggs said, "Civil rights doesn't resolve nothing. [sic.] Black Power is revolutionary and will lay the basis for creating a new social order and a new Constitutional law and order in this country." He said Black Power is a force "repu-diating all existing law and order in this society where the existing Constitutional order is mere police and military con-trol."

James Boggs said the Black Power forces would force the present power structure in America to "increase militia and police" beyond its capacity by bringing the struggle "not to a few cities" but to 20 cities in 1968. He said there would be "military battles" in those cities. Addressing himself directly to the Socialist professors, Boggs said, "There is no in-between. You are either with the revolution or you are not. The United States as a nation is a counter-revolution."

James Boggs said the Black Power revolution is talking "a language the American people don't understand and say they won't understand, but that they've got to be made to understand." He said, "All revolutions start with a minority, from Haiti on down. I don't think over 3 percent of the Russians were ready for the revolution." He said that despite the Black Power forces being representative of a minority in America, "I always visualize that we're going to split the forces of the majority or we're going to have a real vendetta!"

WOULD TEAR DOWN PRESENT SYSTEM

Ivanhoe Donaldson of "Snick" declared, "The struggle of the 60's isn't the ballot or having jobs—it is a physical struggle." He said about the present social and governmental structure in the United States, "Our position is—tear it down because we don't want to be a part of it!" Donaldson said, "In Detroit we defeated the police and the National Guard." He said the riots in Newark and Detroit put a strain on existing police and military forces within the communities and in the United States, and that in 1968 "two or three Detroits at the same time are going to pin down the American forces."

Donaldson said that in the struggle in 10 or 20 cities "next year," the revolutionary forces would not be confined to burning down the black areas, that the forces would "go downtown" and "begin to burn down the white ghetto banks and ghetto draft centers." He said, "There's a Chase Manhattan Bank at 125th Street in this town. We're trying to get jobs in a bank we ought to destroy."

Since that pronouncement, several branches of the Chase Manhattan Bank in New York City have been bombed; a branch of the Bank of America was totally destroyed at Isla Vista, California, in the February 1970 riot there; and a Bank of America branch was bombed in New York City on July 27, 1970.

GUERRILLA WARFARE IN CITIES

At the Socialist Scholars Conference in September 1967, Boggs and Donaldson explained why urban areas in the United States are more favorable to success of guerrilla

Atty. William Kunstler, who represented the "Chicago Seven" in their conspiracy trial, speaks to some 2,000 students at the football field at the University of California at Santa Barbara. Kunstler's scheduled appearance was blamed for the violence which occured late on 2/24/70 in the area. UPI warfare than the countryside, unlike conditions in Cuba and elsewhere. They explained in coldly calculated terms that from the strategic military point of view, guerrilla warfare is much more likely to be successful in the cities where a combination of "violence, sabotage and traffic tie-ups can bring down the system."

From the floor, a questioner asked Ivanhoe Donaldson, "When do we start a guerrilla war?"

James Boggs grabbed the microphone and said, "If he started to answer that, I'd shut his mouth!"

Another questioner asked Boggs whether he believes blacks and whites can ever live together in our nation.

James Boggs, Socialist Scholars Conference panel chairman, replied, "The whites have to struggle against another set of whites and the struggle will be equally as violent." He meant, of course, that white revolutionaries will combat white counter-revolutionaries.

That was the end of the Sunday morning meeting, which lasted for more than two and a half hours. As soon as Boggs had officially adjourned the meeting, he announced over a microphone that another Black Power meeting would take place immediately in the Morgan Room at the New York Hilton "to plan how to do things now and next year."

A fair-haired young girl went up to the dais, told him how wonderful he was, and said, "Aren't you afraid they'll assassinate you?"

Boggs shrugged his shoulders. "No," he said. "I'm not. They don't want to make no martyrs." He paused and a slow smile spread over his face. "Besides," he said deliberately, emphasizing each word, "I'm a scholar, not a leader."

A gray-haired woman in a brown dress said, "Did you say we're meeting in the Morgan Room?"

"Morgan Room is right," he answered. "But not 'we.' Our meeting is for blacks only."

A tall professorial looking man stepped up and asked something. "Sorry," Boggs said. "I'm catching a plane at four o'clock. I've been to Cleveland and Columbus. They put us down in Cleveland last time. But I'm riding out to the airport with someone who's going to tell me how we can fix it so they won't be able to next time."

Next time.
The fire next time.

PLANNED RIOTS

In mid-summer 1970, the riot fires were burning in Miami and Houston, in Asbury Park and New Brunswick, New Jersey, in Lawrence, Kansas and Los Angeles. In Chicago, at a rock music festival on July 27, there was a planned riot in which 162 persons were injured, among whom 126, that is, about 75%, were policemen. The riot spread into the central business district where window-smashing and looting took place.

In the new book *The Riot Makers* by Eugene H. Methvin, there is an exhaustive study of the violent outbreaks in our nation during the 1960's. The study shows conclusively that those whom Mr. Methvin describes as "totalitarian world changers" are responsible for fomenting and prolonging the riots. "They are totalitarian destroyers, demolitionists," writes Mr. Methvin, and he recognizes that they are filled with hate.

I know they are. I know too that they are careful, shrewd and effective planners. In fact, I sat among them, a month after the Third Annual Conference of Socialist Scholars, when they planned the violent disruption of the 1968 Democratic National Convention.

Chapter 9

CONVENTION DISORDERS
PLANNED

ON THE NIGHT of October 17, 1967, I attended a fateful New Politics meeting in Schermerhorn Hall at Columbia University. There I learned about the plans being made for the violence and disruption that would take place ten months later at the 1968 Democratic National Convention in Chicago.

I not only found out about it, I wrote about it a month later in a column which appeared in many newspapers.

There was good reason for my postponing immediate comment about what would happen at the Democratic Convention. In the news business, we generally deal with first things first. The New Politics meeting at Columbia lasted for several hours and was divided into two parts: the first part dealt with the huge demonstration "March on the Pentagon", scheduled to take place four days later in Washington over the weekend of October 21 and 22; the second part of the New Politics meeting dealt with the 1968 Democratic National Convention. Since the first part was so imminent, I wrote about it in the middle of the night on my return home from Schermerhorn Hall, trying to inform the public that the Communist Party was the controlling force behind the forthcoming March on the Pentagon sponsored by Communist David Dellinger, Rennie Davis, and the National Mobilization Committee To End The War in Vietnam, "Mobe."

Under the dateline New York City, October 17, 1967, I reported that at the New Politics meeting, Laird Cummings, who described himself as "a New York business man," acted as temporary chairman, but the real chairman, to whom Cummings constantly referred and deferred, was John J. Abt, member of the National Committee for New Politics and lawyer for the Communist Party, U.S.A. (He is the lawyer whom John F. Kennedy's assassin called for when arrested in Dallas.)

COMMUNIST LEADER IN CONTROL

Abt's first remarks were a call for "action" at the Pentagon. In response, several members of the militant "Resistance" group discussed their strategy for forcing their way up the Pentagon steps and forcing the Army to use force against them. Specific addresses in New York City were designated as places of rendezvous "only for those willing to take part in direct action." Members were told, "You be there and we guarantee to get you there" — meaning, of course, to provide transportation to Washington, D.C.

In his program for organization of the New Politics group, John Abt suggested "a flexible structure with ten or more members in each congressional district to badger every candidate and put him on the spot." He warned them not to reveal their true political purpose by using the slogan "Dump Johnson!" at this stage, saying it was "premature," and told them to wait until after January 1968 to use it.

Again and again during the long session, Laird Cummings said, "The chair calls on Mr. Abt," and John Abt would enter and control the discussion.

The meeting decided to organize demonstrations two weeks after October 21 at local boards of election. The demonstrations took place in November as scheduled and the New York police made many arrests. A month later, on December 8, 1967, Laird Cummings himself was arrested for "harassment" of police officers during a mass demonstration at the U.S. Army Induction Center in Manhattan.

"NEW LEFT" A COMMUNIST DEVICE

On the night of October 17, 1967, I concluded my column on the Schermerhorn Hall meeting as follows:

"When Americans watch TV newscasts on Saturday night and read Sunday morning headlines, October 21 and 22, they probably won't see John J. Abt in the streets of Washington, D.C. or at the Pentagon. But he was on center stage at the 'action' meeting at Columbia University on October 17 that planned for trouble in our nation's capital. His dominant presence at the meeting ought to explode the myth that there is such a thing as the New Left.

"Fellow Americans, the New Left is nothing but a deceptive political technique of the Old Left, meaning the Communist Party, U.S.A. The only new things about the New Left are the youths who are ensnared and the slogans that are coined, such as 'Immediate unconditional withdrawal of U.S. forces from Vietnam' and 'Black Power!'

"I predict that over the weekend of October 21 and 22, when many U.S. embassies will be attacked and when U.S. Armed Forces will have to bar approaches to the Pentagon or be forced to use force against demonstrators there, the American public will at long last wake up to the true significance of Laird Cummings' 'The chair calls on Mr. Abt.'

"By Monday, October 23, no American in his or her right mind will be able to deny that there is a Communist threat to our nation, internally and internationally.'"

I was right about the necessity of our armed forces being forced to use force against violent demonstrators at the Pentagon — action televised in ugliest scenes — but I was wrong about public awakening to Communists' direction of the "peace" demonstration. The awakening would have taken place, and might have prevented future tragedy, had the people been told the truth.

But they were not.

INFORMATION WITHHELD BY OFFICIALS

In a brief news item on an inside page, the *New York Times* reported, October 20, 1967, that Secretary of State Dean Rusk had told a group of New York business executives that the Johnson Administration had decided *not* to tell Americans about Communist control of the "peace" movement in the United States. Secretary Rusk said the U.S. Government has detailed intelligence about that Communist control, and he went on to say, "We haven't made public the extent of our knowledge. We didn't want to set off a new McCarthyism."

That decision, in my opinion, was based on exceedingly poor judgment. In history there always is an event that marks a turning point. The Johnson Administration's decision not to tell the people the truth about the subversion in our midst made certain the downfall of that Administration and created the Identification Gap. It led directly to disunity and confusion among the majority of Americans, who sensed the real situation but were given no factual information by the one source they would have believed and trusted, the President of the United States.

Had President Johnson informed the people about the "detailed intelligence" on Communist subversion that he possessed, he would have been able to unify Americans, among whom the vast majority are anti-Communist, and he never would have been forced to let the Communists and their followers brag that they were able to force the President of the United States "to abdicate."

Still more important, the Johnson Administration's lack of candor with the people on the subject of Communist and Marxist influence in our country showed basic lack of confidence in our good judgment and fairness. In fearing that by telling us the truth they would create "a wave of McCarthyism" (as Secretary Rusk later put it), President Johnson and Secretary Rusk and U.S. Attorney General Ramsey Clark, who received reliable information from the Federal Bureau of Investigation and from other legally constituted intelligence agencies, unintentionally or mistakenly created a sea of confusion that gave rise to the wave of anarchy and violent disruption threatening to engulf the nation.

If the Marxist teachers of destruction were reliably identified by our government for what they are, they would be isolated and unable to attract dupes, misguided young idealists, muddle-headed followers and well-intentioned but unenlightened supporters. Wholly aware of the anti-Marxist sentiments of most Americans, the radical Marxists and

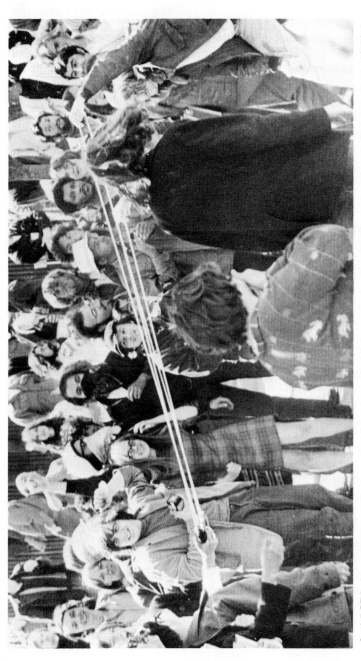

Anti-ROTC demonstrators set up a catapult—a huge slingshot—to hurl rocks at police on campus at Berkeley, Calif. 4/28/70. Earlier a "Peace Brigade" of students headed off a band of militants attempting to storm the Naval ROTC building. UPI

Communists fear exposure of their true political and ideological affiliation more than anything else, for they know that whenever they are identified for what they really are, they can attract only a handful of easily discredited and thwarted adherents.

Sooner or later, though, the truth about the Marxist teachers and planners of destruction in our nation will come out. No news management or unwise decisions by persons in high official places can keep it suppressed forever. In my opinion, however, if the truth continues to be suppressed for much longer, and if violent demonstrations continue to take place, and if the facts about the real origin of that violence continue to be twisted, concealed or deliberately withheld, then chaos will inevitably ensue. For if the present public confusion about who is who and what is what in our country continues, it will lead to unreasoning and blind mob action on the lowest level with most tragic harm to the innocent as well as the guilty in street fighting and a blood bath. Under such conditions, our traditional free government could not survive.

EXPOSE TEACHERS OF DESTRUCTION!

The only non-violent way to prevent future mob action in our multiracial society is for responsible government leaders enjoying access to reliable intelligence information to expose the Marxist teachers of destruction and professional hate-mongers in our nation, and for Congress to control them by means of enlightened internal security legislation supported by the Supreme Court.

A private citizen or writer can only do so much in trying to furnish the public with needed information, no matter how hard he or she tries. And, Heaven knows, I myself have tried!

For a month after the demonstration at the Pentagon in October 1967, I waited and hoped for a change of mind in the Johnson Administration about its decision not to tell the public what it knew from intelligence sources about the violent New Politics agitation in our nation. When I became convinced that the decision would not be changed, either for fear of the charge of "McCarthyism," or in the mistaken illusion that the radical Left could be pacified, wooed and won over by a liberal-oriented Democratic Party, I wrote a newspaper column about the second part of the New Politics meeting at Schermerhorn Hall, Columbia University, October 17, the part that planned and organized in almost every detail the violence that took place at the 1968 Democratic National Convention, including the Communist-coined slogan to be shouted into TV sound equipment, "The whole world is watching."

PREDICTED LONG IN ADVANCE

Datelined New York City, November 28, 1967, and marked "exclusive," the column ran in client papers as follows:

"Pentagon Prelude to Democratic Convention

"It would be wise for President Johnson to inform the public about the details of Communist participation in the October 21 demonstration at the Pentagon, because it was only a Red prelude to what Communists and New Leftists are planning to stage at the Democratic Convention in Chicago at the International Amphitheater next August.

"As chief executive, the President certainly has the right not to divulge the contents of any intelligence report prepared for him on events at the Pentagon over the weekend of October 21-22. But it would be helpful for the President to give the public a personal summary of present day Communist aims, strategy and tactics in our nation. In that way, the public will be better able to put into true perspective the coming fracas at the Democratic Convention in Chicago.

"If all goes according to the radical leftists' present plans, there will be riotous scenes inside the hall and at the entrances and exits. In order for the Democratic Convention to proceed in an orderly way, it probably will be necessary to surround the hall, just as the Pentagon was surrounded, by police, guardsmen and riot control units of the armed forces. Plans for disrupting the convention were discussed at a meeting of members of the New York Chapter of the National

Conference for New Politics at Schermerhorn Hall, Columbia University, Oct. 17, only four days before the Pentagon demonstration.

"The meeting was presided over by temporary chairman Laird Cummings and was politically dominated by John Abt, a lawyer for the Communist Party, U.S.A., and by Seymour Copstein, identified as 'a Communist' during the Rapp— Coudert investigations of Communist infiltration of the New York public school system.

"Present at the meeting in Schermerhorn Hall were Florence Kennedy and other militant Harlem leaders of the 'Black Power' movement. They said openly, 'If the Mississippi Freedom Democratic Party convention delegates are not the Mississippi delegation, then there won't be any Mississippi delegation. We'll block the entrances and exits and there won't be a Democratic Convention. There won't be any compromise like last time.'

"Chairman Cummings recognized a speaker from the floor who said, 'Johnson thinks Chicago was a smart choice because he thinks the Daley machine and police have got things under control there. He'll find out that Chicago was a dumb choice, because we'll have things the way we want them.'

"There were shouts of 'You said it!'

"A tall woman in an orange dress explained how the Mississippi Freedom Democratic Party headquarters in Clarksdale, Miss., would be run. 'The money and political direction will be coming from those right here in this room,' she said. 'The activities will be centered down there. Without our money and our direction, they can't function. Activities at the Chicago convention have got to be centered on the MFDP and Vietnam issues.'

"Mr. Copstein said there should not be overemphasis on the Vietnam issue because President Johnson might take some action there that would pull the rug out from under the anti-Vietnam agitation. Copstein said the NCNP should keep in mind the class struggle issue. . . .

"John Abt said that strategy and tactics for the Democratic convention should be discussed at further NCNP meetings. Several speakers mentioned 'disruption' of the convention and boasted that the forthcoming demonstration at the Pentagon would serve as valuable experience in testing tactics for Chicago next August where 'a real showdown' could be achieved. They bragged that 'the authorities' use of force against us will prove there's no such thing as democratic elections in the imperialist United States.' Undoubtedly, the Leftists and Communists will stage riotous demonstrations in Chicago so that TV films of the scenes will be shown everywhere in the world as means of Communist propaganda to discredit our American electoral process.

"The Pentagon demonstration of last October 21 was only a trial run for the demonstrations at the Democratic Convention in Chicago next August. The same radicals and Communists who took part in the first will take part in the second disgraceful propaganda effort against our country. That is why it would be wise for President Johnson to brief the public on the facts about who organized and directed the Pentagon demonstration. Forewarned is forearmed."

To try to forewarn the people of Mississippi about the direction, political control and funding by Communists in New York City of the Mississippi Freedom Democratic Party, and what the MFDP would try to do at the 1968 Democratic Convention, I sent the foregoing column to several newspapers in that state, papers not on my regular list. Not a single Mississippi paper even acknowledged receipt of the information.

I know this: If Mayor Daley and the Chicago Police had not enforced such strict security inside the Democratic Convention hall (a security so much objected to by members of the press in attendance, some out of ignorance, a few out of complicity in that planning), there would have been the same violence, destruction and bloodshed inside the International Amphitheater as outside in the Chicago streets.

In New York City, as early as October 1967, that is what the New Politics group planned for Chicago in August 1968. Had the violence outside been brought into the hall, the entire electoral process in our nation would have been impaired and perhaps destroyed.

Chapter 10

REDUCING COLLEGES

...To Centers of Revolution

IN OUR COUNTRY in 1968, the radical revolutionary planning for violence and destruction went on and on, with almost no serious attention paid to it by the press and by responsible government officials and academic leaders. As usual, I was the only reporter present at New York University, over the weekend of February 10-11, 1968, when Students for a Democratic Society held a regional conference to help plan SDS' program for ten days of violence and disruption in our American communities during April 21-April 30.

Formal notice of a forthcoming February regional SDS conference at New York University was published in *Firebomb,* the SDS daily newsletter, which stated:

"An organization like ours takes a major step forward when it finally comes to understand that it is involved in a struggle against an enemy and takes major steps toward confronting that enemy head-on. A serious organization consciously seeking to develop a revolutionary practice creates a life-or-death dynamic within the society it is trying to destroy and recreate. . . ."

The *Firebomb* editorial went on to say that the "ten days in April" program gave SDS members "a vehicle for pulling our organization together as a real political force in America. . .We've got from now until April to organize the hell out of this city. Then we open up and confront the power structure and the people, and if we survive the confrontation we organize some more. At the same time, our brothers and sisters will be pulling themselves together all over the country."

IMITATE BOLSHEVIKS

To what end did this pulling together take place? The answer is: To carry out an SDS program in April described by members as "Ten Days To Shake the Empire." By "empire" the SDS members meant "the United States." Their slogan was taken from John Reed's description of the Bolshevik Revolution in Russia as "Ten Days That Shook The World."

Almost every word uttered at the SDS meeting in a subcellar games room at Weinstein Residence Hall, New York University, Saturday afternoon, February 10th, was Moscow-oriented and predicated historically on the Bolshevik Revolution in Russia.

Steve Halliwell of SDS at Columbia University was a main speaker. He urged his listeners to become like the revolutionary students at universities in Russia during "the pre-Lenin period." An overall theme of SDS was that 1968 could be "the 1905" of the American revolution. What the radical students meant is that they knew they could not bring down the American government as soon as 1968, but they expected that their violent revolutionary activities, even though put down that year, would force the police to use force against the students and thus create resentment against our government in the same manner as the unsuccessful Marxist-inspired Russian revolution of 1905 did against the Czarist regime.

It is ridiculous for news analysts and TV commentators to pin their discussion of radical Marxist organizations, such as Students for a Democratic Society, on the terms "New Left" and "Old Left." The so-called "New Left" has been shaped and indoctrinated by the "Old Left" just as young Communist Bettina Aptheker was fathered by aging Communist Herbert Aptheker, Eugene Dennis, Jr., a founder of the first campus W.E.B. DuBois Club at the University of Wisconsin in 1964, is the son of Eugene Dennis, onetime national secretary of the Communist Party, U.S.A., and current fugitive from justice Kathy Boudin, SDS Weatherman member, is the daughter of Leonard B. Boudin, long-time pro-Communist lawyer. Naturally, many present-day circumstances are different from those of a generation and more ago, but the basic ideology and revolutionary tactics used by Bolsheviks, terrorists, and anarchists in Europe and the United States more than sixty years ago are exactly like those used today by radicals, youthful Leftist terrorists and anarchists in our country and elsewhere.

The official agenda of the SDS New York regional conference, at New York University, included in part:

"Saturday February 10:

"10:00 general meeting, subcellar, Weinstein Residence Hall, University Place between 8th St. and Waverly Place; presentation of papers on spring program with open floor discussion. Bob Tomashevsky, chairman.

"Sunday, February 11:

"Women's liberation; American Room, 2 Washington Square North (basement); led by Naomi Jaffe and Bernardine Dohrn, Sue Shargell.

"MDS* (society of elders): room 11, 2 Washington Square North, led by Marge Piercy.

"High School Program: location to be announced; led by Judy Berezin, Trudy Bennet, John Moore.

"Transit Strike: . . . led by Leif Johnson and Steve Kromm. .,. ."

It is impossible to report verbatim on most of what was said at the SDS meeting on Saturday afternoon in the steamheated, poorly ventilated subcellar of Weinstein Hall. The language was as foul as the stench of the two hundred students there, most of whom were physically filthy. Outdoors the weather was bitter cold. Indoors, the students took off coats and heavy sweaters, leaving them piled on the floor in heaps that stank like the tons of uncollected garbage piled high on city streets. Both male and female students used the kind of filthy speech that GI's disdainfully describe as "latrine talk." It is incredible that any institute of higher

---

*Movement for a Democratic Society

Gas-masked policeman throws a tear gas canister into a crowd 4/29/70 after violence erupted on the Ohio State University Campus (Columbus, Ohio). Over 25 persons, including police, were injured, six were shot. Nearly 100 persons were arrested.   UPI

learning in our country would permit such debasement of our language on the premises without interruption and strongest possible remonstrance from a faculty member or administrator.

UNIVERSITY AUTHORITY FAILED TO SUPERVISE

Not knowing whether any such representative was indeed present at the SDS subcellar meeting, I later inquired at the office of Chancellor Allan M. Cartter of New York University and was referred to Mr. Robert Terte, of the NYU News Bureau, who stated, "It is not university practice to supervise meetings sponsored by duly constituted student groups."

The reply brings up the question of whether university trustees, directors and administrators should tolerate Students for a Democratic Society as a "duly constituted" student group. Officially, SDS moved onward from a policy of dissent to one of "resistance." The kind of Resistance advocated by SDS is illegal activity designed to destroy the existing university system in our nation and to destroy the U.S. government. If university authorities are willing to tolerate violent revolutionary groups on campus, then it seems that the universities' policy of no supervision over student political and activist groups ought to be changed.

No college or university today can afford to adopt a policy of absolute *laissez faire* on campus. Any university that does pursue such a policy toward student groups is bound to tolerate on its premises the kind of criminal plotting and planning that went on in the subcellar of Weinstein Hall on February 10. A university administration that washes its hands of all responsibility for supervision of such a meeting is an administration totally in the dark about the subversive activities of its own student body. A university administration that remains absent from an SDS regional conference taking place on campus is an administration that will sooner or later be forced to come to grips with the kind of illegal student activity which necessitates police intervention.

In the article about the SDS meeting at Weinstein Hall which was published in my own *U.S.A. Magazine*, March 1, 1968, and was reprinted on the front page of *Barron's* under the title "Ten Days in April" on March 11, 1968, I reported:

"Throughout our country today there is argument over whether university administrators should or should not 'call in the police' during illegal student demonstrations. From April 21 to April 30, 1968, it is highly probable that administrators in dozens of universities will have to summon the police to suppress violent resistance to authority, law and order plotted by Students for a Democratic Society and its affiliates, such as the W.E.B. DuBois Clubs.

"There is no group in our society which ought to be more devoted to upholding the civilized traditions of law and order than university trustees, directors and administrators. They have no right to enjoy a privileged status among the population, a status isolating them from civic and social responsibility."

At the SDS subcellar meeting at New York University, February 10 and 11, 1968, there was distributed a position paper — "Toward a Political Resistance" by Ian McMahan of Brooklyn College SDS, and by Joe Grossman, Mike Reuss, Carol Rosenbaum, Miriam Snider and Jim West of N.Y.U. SDS. Among statements in the position paper are:

"In the last year or so, the movement has come from dissent to resistance. We have organized in local communities and on campus, and we have engaged in ever more militant demonstrations. . . .

"The movement in California has already won an incredible victory in this direction. Spearheaded by the same activists who organized the Oakland Induction Center confrontation, the Peace and Freedom Party has organized over 105,000 people across the state into local clubs. Most of these are new people, entering politics for the first time. . . . The recent PFP demonstration against Rusk in San Francisco was met by police clubs. In Oakland the PFP is working closely with the Black Panther Party in a campaign to save Black Panther leader Huey Newton, who is in jail on a murder rap for allegedly shooting a cop. . . ."

In the subcellar at Weinstein Hall at New York University, February 10, 1968, the SDS plenary session was addressed by Gerry Tenney who, a year earlier, was a main organizer of the SDS Radical Education Project regional conference at Princeton University, also unattended by an adult supervisor. At N.Y.U. as at Princeton, Tenney urged SDS members to work for "control" over the universities.

WOULD DESTROY UNIVERSITIES

Definitely, the most important thing at colleges and universities today is the matter of control. If administrators and trustees remain in ignorance of conspiracies against their control, then they, and the parents to whom they are responsible for the education of students, will lose control and the university as we know it will be destroyed.

On Saturday afternoon at the New York University SDS conference, a young woman with long straight blonde hair and strong southern accent declared she was protesting to educational authorities her dismissal "last week" from her teaching job at a Brooklyn college. "I was merely furnishing drugs to those of my students who wanted them," she declared, and then called for a "cadre" of five SDS volunteers to meet with her and Harlem Black Power leader Florence Kennedy "to help educate some of my students."

No sooner had she finished her remarks than copies of *Spark*—a monthly publication issued by SDS at Long Island University—were distributed in the subcellar. To make clear the origin of the name, there was scribbled in chalked Cyrillic alphabet letters on the subcellar walls and floors the Russian word for "spark" —*"uckpa"*— which, pronounced phonetically in English, is "eeskrah." That was the name of the Bolshevik publication edited by Lenin during all his years of exile from Russia in the early 20th century.

REVOLUTIONARY ACTIVITIES

There was also distributed at the SDS meeting at New York University a "research paper" by the North American Congress on Latin America (NACLA), an organization seeking to impair U.S. good relations with Latin American nations. NACLA is doing a smear job on every big U.S. corporation with investments in Latin America and on all our diplomatic missions to the area. There is reason to believe that NACLA members are carrying out pro-Communist intelligence work in Latin America and are in contact with Communist guerrilla leaders there. The SDS newsletter *Firebomb* announced that at the N.Y.U. regional SDS conference "A paper on intelligence work prepared by NACLA will be distributed." But when the conference opened, SDS leaders at registration headquarters said, "It was decided to withhold the NACLA paper because it gives away too much."

It certainly must have given away a lot about NACLA's subversive work, because SDS members are not at all shy about disclosing their nefarious schemes. If the paper could be found, it might give away a clue to the possible whereabouts of NACLA member Pat Swinton, wanted by the F.B.I. on charges of having taken part in the bombings of private and public buildings in New York City, November 1969. Investigation of NACLA, and of its members' cooperation with members of the Communist-controlled Committee of Returned Volunteers, all former Peace Corps workers, might also furnish clues to how Communist guerrillas in some Latin American countries have been able to kidnap some of our diplomatic personnel there while on the way to appointments or recreational activity.

Another paper presented at the N.Y.U. SDS meeting in Weinstein Hall subcellar, February 1968, was by Steve Halliwell, then a member of Columbia University SDS. He proposed a violent confrontation with police in the financial district of New York City, with demonstrations against IBM, the First National City Bank, Chase Manhattan Bank and Socony Mobil Corporation. In 1969 and 1970, each of those institutions was the target of violence.

In the beginning of March 1968, my article about the SDS subcellar meeting at New York University ended with the following paragraphs:

"In these changing times, it seems the better part of plain common sense for college and university trustees and

Striking Rutgers University, New Brunswick, N.J. students cheer as Rutgers President, Dr. Mason W. Gross, on 5/4/70 announces his support for the student strike, and recommends that the faculty strike also. The students are protesting U.S. involvement in Cambodia. UPI

administrators to change existing rules and set up strict supervision over on-campus student activities. The present hands-off policy is not one of genuine adherence to the First Amendment, it is one of *laissez faire* leading to violent abuse of academic and civic freedom.

"If Students for a Democratic Society members are permitted to carry out their planned ten-day program of violent resistance in April, with accompanying bloodshed, then an outraged and angry American public will fix the blame where it belongs, on university trustees, directors and administrators. They should act now and announce that any student taking part in any illegal activity will be instantly expelled.

"The recent SDS regional conference in New York University was a disgrace to that institution and an outrage against the citizenry. From coast to coast, Americans should demand that university administrators get control over their own institutions or get out. Otherwise, student subversion, abetted in some instances by faculty members, can eventually accomplish its aim and bring down our free American university system and free U.S. Government."

Immediately after the SDS subcellar meeting at New York University in February 1968, I wrote two newspaper columns about the coming SDS-led campus rebellions scheduled for the period April 21-April 30, and the long article "Ten Days in April" published by *Barron's* on March 11. Not a single administrator, faculty member, alumnus or trustee at Columbia University made any effort to seek additional information from me.

Many readers of my columns and article did send letters of inquiry to New York University. Its administrators did not request further first-hand information from me and claimed that I had either misunderstood or exaggerated what went on in Weinstein subcellar. But I hadn't misunderstood, not even the Russian revolutionary slogan "spark" (ees-krah) that was scrawled in red Cyrillic letters on the walls and floor of Weinstein Hall subcellar and, two months later, was splashed in red paint on the walls of ransacked offices at Columbia University and on stone steps, doors and monuments there.

After the violent and destructive SDS-led rebellion broke out right on schedule at Columbia University, however, I was besieged with inquiries from the big news wire services, from editors across the nation, and from Columbia University faculty members, students and alumni.

The chancellor and assistant chancellor of New York University kept mum and made no move to supervise SDS, or prevent SDS-fomented trouble at N.Y.U., until the university library there was set afire the following year and the administration had to call on the police for help in imposing a discipline that should have been enforced long before.

Had there been inquiries from administrators at Columbia or N.Y.U. in February and March, 1968, I could have told them about the violently revolutionary and incendiary remarks made in Weinstein Hall by Ted Gold, vice-chairman of Columbia SDS, who invaded Low Library with Mark Rudd on March 27, staged an illegal sit-in there, and was put on probation by Columbia, a mild disciplinary move that proved to be utterly meaningless, because Ted Gold, along with Steve Halliwell and Mark Rudd, was a main activist in the bloody violence on the Columbia campus in April.

When Ted Gold was dynamited to bits, March 6, 1970, in the house on West 11th Street in Manhattan, a luxurious private home which he and other SDS Weathermen had turned into a bomb factory, I was shocked but not surprised, having listened to him voice his explosive views not only in Weinstein Hall subcellar at New York University but also at a "Pretty Boy Floyd" lecture held by SDS "elders" in the Movement for a Democratic Society, October 3, 1968, at the cafeteria in the New School. There Ted Gold solicited recruits for the radical Teachers for a Democratic Society.

GRAND JURY FINDINGS

Another figure present at the Weinstein Hall subcellar meeting at N.Y.U. was Bernardine Dohrn, who led the discussion on "women's liberation." She was one of 13 persons indicted by a Federal grand jury in Detroit on July 23, 1970 on charges of conspiring to bomb and kill.

The indictment charges:

"It was part of the conspiracy that the defendants and the unindicted co-conspirators, together with others not known to the grand jury, would organize a 'central committee' to direct underground bombing operations of the defendants and co-conspirators; that this group would be assigned to Berkeley, Calif.; Chicago, Ill.; New York, N.Y.; and Detroit, Mich.; that clandestine and underground 'focals,' consisting of three or four persons, would be established; that the 'focals' would be commanded by the 'central committee' in the bombing of police and other civic, business and educational buildings throughout the country."

The Detroit grand jury charges that members of the "focals" would travel around the country using false identities and communicating through coded messages, obtain firearms and explosives, and use them to bomb police and other buildings and kill and injure those inside.

The 13 indicted persons are: Mark Rudd, 23 years old; Bernardine Dohrn, 27; William Ayers, 25; Kathy Boudin, 27; Linda Evans, 23; Cathy Wilkerson, 25; Dianne Donghi, 21; Russell Neufeld, 22; Jane Spielman, 23; Ronald Fliegelman, 26; Larry Grathwohl, 22; Naomi Jaffe, 27; and Robert Burlingham, 24.

Named in the indictment as a co-conspirator but not defendant is the dead Ted Gold. Defendant Bernardine Dohrn is a fugitive from justice.

Surely it is plain to all now, exactly as I reported in February and March 1968, that campus subversion — mainly instigated by members of the Socialist Scholars and other Marxist teachers of destruction — threatens to "bring down our free American university system and free U.S. Government."

In statement after statement to President Nixon's Commission on Campus Unrest, witnesses have testified that many students developed a hatred in general for our American society. Why not? For years, that hatred has been inculcated by the merciless Marxist criticism of almost every aspect of our society in the teachings and writings of professors such as the pro-Communist Corliss Lamont at Columbia University, and of Professors Seymour Melman, Alexander Erlich and Richard A. Cloward, all Socialist Scholars on the Columbia faculty.

SO THEY ORGANIZE FOR MORE DESTRUCTION

Had President Grayson Kirk of Columbia University acted with much greater firmness, and had he quickly imposed strict discipline on the student body as soon as the April 1968 rebellion broke out there, it is probable that the subsequent insurrections at Harvard, Cornell, Stanford, Ohio State and other institutions of higher learning would not have taken place. As SDS proclaimed in the *Firebomb* advance notice of the February 1968 meeting in Weinstein Hall at New York University, "we open up and confront the power structure and the people, and if we survive the confrontation we organize some more."

SDS and the Socialist Scholars organization did survive the April 1968 confrontation at Columbia. So they did "organize some more." The rebellion at Columbia was the testing ground and the organizing went on and on.

In 1968, Bernardine Dohrn went from New York University to the campus at Kent State University, Ohio, where she distributed the SDS pamphlet "The War Is On At Kent State" and with other SDS members and Marxist faculty members laid the groundwork for the terrible events that took place there two years later in the spring of 1970.

By July 14, 1968, the late Chesly Manly reported in the *Chicago Tribune* that Richard Flacks, an assistant professor of sociology at the University of Chicago, and Robert Ross, a graduate student there, were forming a new organization, the New University Conference, to enable graduate students and faculty members "to lend organized support to student rebellions" — as Robert Ross put it.

Billions of words have been written about the Columbia University rebellion of April 1968. Millions and millions of dollars have been spent on committees of inquiry into campus violence. Presidents Johnson and Nixon appointed commissions to study it. Hundreds of academicians and sociologists have been called on to testify whether in their opinion the April 1968 rebellion at Columbia and the August 1968 riots at the Democratic National Convention in Chicago were the results of "a conspiracy."

There is no need, in my opinion, to delve into such a complicated and time-consuming discussion. It is simpler and more accurate to say they were planned by Marxist teachers of destruction and their followers and pupils. I was present among the planners when they made their plans. Almost all, sad to say, were carried out.

CHAPTER 11

TEACHERS AS FUSE,
STUDENTS AS DETONATORS

THE REVEREND William Sloane Coffin, Jr., chaplain of Yale University, was host at a luncheon for more than two hundred members of the Leftist "in" crowd at the Hotel Roosevelt Terrace Room in New York City, July 9, 1968.

The formal invitation to the affair read: "Reverend William Sloane Coffin, Jr., on behalf of Clergy and Laymen Concerned About Vietnam, and American Documentary Films, cordially invites you to be his guest at a luncheon on Tuesday, July 9th. . . . Mr. David Schoenbrun will speak on the Paris peace negotiations. His talk will be filmed by American Documentary Films for distribution throughout the United States. RSVP to American Documentary Films—799-7440."

It is unusual for a formal invitation to give only a telephone number for social response. As a matter of fact, there were many unusual aspects of the Coffin luncheon, which was attended by clergymen, professors, graduate students, members of Women Strike for Peace and of the militant National Black Anti-Draft, Anti-War Union.

At cocktails before lunch, there was much conversation about the end of "phase one" of Leftists' operations in our nation. "We forced the President of the United States to abdicate," was an oft-repeated boast, followed by a toast to "our victory at Columbia." The victory of the student rebellion at Columbia University, they meant.

In unguarded conversation during cocktails before Coffin's luncheon, only one aspect of the upcoming phase two in their operations was mentioned by guests. "We're going to take the student movement out of the hands of the undergraduates and put it in the hands of politically sophisticated, better disciplined graduate students," a dynamic young woman from Rutgers University told a group of listeners. "We have some good ones at Stanford and Chicago. We've brought some good foreign ones in through Fulbright scholarships."

GUERRILLA CINEMA

At lunch, Rev. Coffin introduced Jerry Stoll, president of American Documentary Films, Inc. He described his company as "a non-profit organization" and said it was developing "a distribution apparatus." Mr. Stoll said the company's first film, "Sons and Daughters," which is about the student demonstrations at Berkeley, had been seen by a million people and was designed to educate parents by showing them how they could learn to follow in sons' and daughters' demonstrating footsteps and catch up with social change. Mr. Stoll said his company's second film, "Vietnam", with David Schoenbrun, formerly of CBS, as narrator, had already reached more than 500,000 people. "It has been shown twice to Congressmen in Washington, D.C.," said Stoll. "Senator Fulbright entered it [the script] for us in the Congressional Record."

Guests wanting to learn more about American Documentary Films, Inc., could glance through its literature while having lunch. A statement in the literature said that American Documentary Films copyrighted the name "Guerrilla Cinema" in 1967.

It is a fitting name. As of July 1970, some of the guerrilla cinema films distributed by American Documentary Films, which has offices in New York City and San Francisco, are: "Stagolee," an interview with Bobby Seale of the Black Panther Party; "Eldridge Cleaver Speaks"; "Rubin on Schools" narrated by Jerry Rubin, foul-mouthed member of the Chicago Conspiracy Seven; "One Way To Change The World — Cuba, 1968–1969"; and "Ho Chi Minh." In the current American Documentary Films catalogue, under the heading "RED TAPE," there are listed thirteen audio tapes, among which eight are by and for Black Panthers, and one tape is of an incendiary speech by William Kunstler, lawyer for the Conspiracy Seven, made at Santa Barbara, California, scene of student rioting led by outside agitators, in February 1970, during which a branch of the Bank of America was totally destroyed.

BIAS OF FORMER CBS NARRATOR

As soon as dessert and coffee had been served, klieg lights were turned on and Rev. Coffin introduced the guest seated at his right, Gerhard Elston, whom Rev. Coffin jokingly described as "the Mr. Vietnam of the National Council of Churches." The audience laughed knowingly and heartily. Mr. Elston heaped praise on David Schoenbrun, who went to the microphone, blinked at the powerful lights, acknowledged the loud applause, and launched into an extremely well organized, witty and vicious propaganda attack on United States policy in Vietnam, on American foreign policy, and on American society in general.

Looking very well groomed and prosperous, he pointed the finger of shame at our society in which, he charged, "five per cent of the people own 20 per cent of all the nation's wealth." He reproached the United States for giving only $2 billion a year in foreign aid to the underdeveloped nations while "the Soviet Union is giving $7 billion."

Next day, it happened that the *Wall Street Journal* carried news from Paris on the official report of the Organization for Economic Cooperation and Development (OECD) which states that the net flow of public and private capital from advanced to less-developed nations in 1967 totaled $11.4 billion for the 17 OECD members, and "about $350 million from Communist countries."

Mr. Schoenbrun called for "an immediate cease fire in Vietnam and formation of a coalition communal government."

Though his talk at the Coffin luncheon was announced on the printed invitation as dealing with the Paris peace negotiations, it became clear, as Mr. Schoenbrun went on and on in bitterest, most sarcastic and sharp-tongued dialectical criticism of our country, that the Paris talks and Vietnam issue were not the main ones with which he is concerned. While a four-man American Documentary Films camera crew focused on him, Mr. Schoenbrun launched into a radical tirade. "The main struggle," he said, "is the rich-poor struggle."

In New Deal days, said David Schoenbrun, Americans were poor, frightened and divided. "Now that we got America going again, mostly for white people," he said, "we are rich, divided and frightened." As cameras kept on grinding, he ground out all the current radical Leftist clichés about "10,000,000 starving Americans" and about the rapaciousness of the "military-industrial-university-labor-union-complex" of the Establishment. The punch-line of his filmed speech was, "Remember, Martin Luther King did not preach non-violence, he preached *militant* non-violence."

Reverend William Sloane Coffin's luncheon guests gave David Schoenbrun a standing ovation.

"He really was wonderful, wasn't he?" said a member of Women Strike for Peace. A member of the National Black Anti-Draft, Anti-War Union, Warren Reeves, said he thought the speech was "okay," and added that the only government he approves of is not the Soviet government or U.S. government but the Cuban government. A tall thin clergyman with protruding eyes and teeth smiled at the woman from Women Strike for Peace. "We brought down the man in the White House and the establishment at Columbia," he said, his Adam's apple bobbing up and down over his low ministerial collar "We can bring down the whole system."

The camera lights went off.

Reverend Coffin bade his guests adieu.

Undoubtedly, his luncheon for the Leftist "in" crowd marked for most of the guests the triumphant end of what they describe as "phase one" in their operations.

"See you at Rutgers in September," said several of the Ivy League academic guests to one another as they departed on their separate ways.

Many of them did get together there two months later when the Socialist Scholars held their fourth annual conference at Rutgers University, New Jersey, over the weekend of September 6-8, a conference at which militant young Marxists wearing blue armbands marked "SSC" guarded locked meeting room doors.

AGITATOR FROM ABROAD

The guest of honor was Ernest Mandel of Brussels, editor of the Belgian Socialist weekly *La Gauche* (The Left), who was a main instigator of the student riots and workers' strikes in France, May and June, 1968. Now banned from that country, Mandel made his way into our own via Paris-Havana-Brussels. He was formally introduced by Paul Sweezy, editor of the Leftist radical *Monthly Review,* who said, "Ernest Mandel is one of the most eminent and important Marxist theorists in Europe today. He spent considerable time last summer in Cuba. He was active in events which took place in France last spring and is banned by the French government for his part in those events. We're all hoping he will go back to France and take part in events developing there now."

It is a pity that Mandel's speech at dinner in Neilson Dining Hall, Rutgers, on Friday evening, September 6th, was not broadcast to the American public. He speaks excellent English and received a standing ovation from the Socialist Scholars and their guests, busloads of radical youths from New York City and other centers. Had the public heard what Mandel said, statistics in an opinion poll of approval or disapproval for security and riot control action taken during the 1968 Democratic National Convention would rise to 99.9 per cent in favor of Mayor Daley and the Chicago police. Moreover, if TV networks had featured Mandel's speech, there would be no more confusion among loyal Americans about the revolutionary leadership of violent student rebellions and "peace" demonstrations in our country. Also, there would be much less naiveté in certain liberal press and political circles.

"Students," explained Ernest Mandel, "are the detonators in the formula for triggering off a social explosion creating a revolutionary situation."

To resounding applause, he made clear how he and other socialists use Marxism-Leninism as the device for timing, controlling and targeting the explosion. Mandel said the main strategy for overthrowing neo-capitalism in advanced industrial nations today, including the United States, is "to put forth, through mass strikes and mass movements, concrete demands and goals which are unacceptable to the capitalist system and cannot be granted within the capitalist system."

THREE KEY DEMANDS

The three key issues on which Marxists must make their stand, said Mandel, the issues on which capitalists cannot compromise without forfeiting capitalism, are: (1) workers' control; (2) workers' "self-defense" (meaning armed might); and (3) government by workers' councils instead of bourgeois power.

"Never," cried Mandel dramatically, "never, I assure you, were Frenchmen so free, so truly free, as in the days of May-June!"

Shouts of approval came from the long-haired, bearded youths in Neilson Dining Hall, many of whose faces had stared out of front page news photos during the demonstrations at the Pentagon and Columbia University, at draft-card burnings and in street actions, in attacks on the Chicago police during the 1968 Democratic National Convention. Members of the Old Left attending the dinner—Corliss Lamont, Russ Nixon, Harry Magdoff *et al*—were less vociferous but equally enthusiastic, their faces wreathed in beaming smiles.

When the applause died down, Ernest Mandel quoted a statement by James M. Roche, former president of General Motors, published in a news weekly, September 30, 1967: "We live in a world of change. We work in a world of change."

Television cameraman Lou Calderon sports this protective sheet of plexi-glass attachment on his camera during coverage of latest series of melees at University of California campus (Berkeley) 4/28/70 (TOP). At (BOTTOM) Calderon is down on pavement after he suffered permanent eye damage during conflict on the campus on 4/15/70. A rock smashed the eye-piece of his gas mask and his vision is now blurred. UPI

Smiling sarcastically, Mandel paused a moment to look around the dining hall, then moved to the climax of his speech. "It may seem strange that I would agree on anything with such a person," he said, "but I would accept that statement and amend it a little bit." Slowly and with utmost emphasis, he said that under conditions making it possible for a General Motors to exist, "there is a possibility that the very society will change."

Applauding loudly, the Socialist gathering rose to pay homage to the speaker. Certainly, if they and their associates have their way, our American society will be so changed that no private enterprise can exist. The tenet of their entire weekend conference at Rutgers was that after a social explosion has been detonated in the United States, only a revolutionary organization directed by socialists adhering to an advance Marxist-Leninist plan can exercise successful, decisive leadership. They believe it is the function of Socialist Scholars to formulate the plan and adapt it to given conditions while adhering to basic Marxist-Leninist strategy.

The official program for the Rutgers conference listed the following panel discussion leaders:

Warren Susman, Rutgers University;
Christopher Lasch, Northwestern University;
Herbert Gutman, University of Rochester;
Melvyn Dubofsky, University of Massachusetts, Amherst;
Philip Foner, Lincoln University;
Alexander Erlich, Columbia University;
Eugene D. Genovese, Sir George William University, Montreal;
Sterling Stuckey, Northwestern University;
Alphonse Pinckney, Hunter College;
Harold Cruse, author of *The Crisis of the Negro Intellectual;*
Ann Lane, Douglass College;
Gar Alperovitz, M.I.T.;
Michael Greenberg, Polytechnical Institute of Brooklyn;
Geoff White, Berkeley.

(Programmed but unable to attend were Conor Cruise O'Brien of New York University, who conducted "liberation" classes for rebel students at Columbia, and Louis Salkever of State University of New York at Albany.)

THE ROLE OF "THE INTELLECTUAL"

At the Friday morning session on the role of the intellectual, Christopher Lasch said, "The emergence of a mature American culture depends on the emergence of revolutionary change." He said, "The responsibility of the intellectual is the same as that of the street organizer."

Warren Susman said the primary function of the intellectual is the "ideology-making function," and that revolutionary intellectuals must "turn private problems into social issues and turn desires into systems of value, needs into social goals."

He explained that Karl Marx' "praxis" unites feelings, thought and action; that Marx had "the only solution" and through his genius showed that ours is a world of change, that change can be purposeful, and there is "no conflict between theory and practice."

Christopher Lasch said only a socialist scholar "can be sure of what he's doing."

At the conference, Prof. Eugene D. Genovese discussed "Black Power and Socialism," criticized some aspects of Harold Cruse's book *The Crisis of the Negro Intellectual,* but said the author's "ideological manifesto wiped out decades of ideological drivel." Genovese declared, "Black socialists must be free to address black nationalists." He discussed the latter's problems, attacked American society for using "the same terrorist methods against black nationalism that the Zionist bund uses," and said, "White America must be restructured if Black America is to be free."

Genovese used the exact terminology in the uncensored edition of Joseph Stalin's *Marxism and the National and Colonial Question*, which contains two chapters on the Jewish question, and defines Zionism as "a reactionary, rightist political bund movement." To Leninist-Stalinists, all nationalist movements are "fascist" except those directed by Communists and set up for the sole purpose of leading a nation or minority group into absorption by the Communist bloc. Khrushchev denounced Stalin but affirmed Kremlin adherence to Marxism-Leninism-Stalinism. The present Soviet regime led by Kosygin and Brezhnev sticks rigidly to that ideology, and so does the Gomulka regime of Poland. The Communist attitude toward Zionism has nothing to do with pro- or anti-Semitism, or with pro- or anti-Zionism; the attitude has to do solely with orthodox Marxism-Leninism-Stalinism on the national and colonial question, an attitude now dominating the Soviet Union's *political* moves in the Middle East, and in every other region of the world beyond the borders of the USSR, including Soviet policy on Black nationalism within the United States and in the Caribbean area.

Eugene Genovese stated at the panel on Black Power that there can be no successful "black enclave economy" in the United States. He maintains that only in a worldwide radical Marxist economy can there take place an end to racist exploitation.

GOAL: A SOCIALIST AMERICA

The establishment of such an economy was the theme of the entire Socialist Scholars Conference at Rutgers University during the weekend of September 6–8. The aim — as Warren Susman put it — is "to formulate a revolutionary plan for the future which will remove the power of past traditions and create a Socialist America."

On Saturday morning, Professor Alexander Erlich of Columbia University, who in June 1968 delivered the "anti-commencement" address to rebel student walk-outs from the regular commencement exercises, shared the Socialist Scholars platform at Rutgers with guest of honor Ernest Mandel to discuss "The Working Class and Neo-Capitalism." Prof. Erlich was introduced to the audience by John Cammett of Rutgers, 1967-68 president of the Socialist Scholars, who said about Prof. Erlich, "He is a member of the Russian Institute at Columbia and one of the very few professors to take a constructive role in the student events there."

Erlich speaks English with such a heavy accent it was difficult to hear and understand what he said. The poor acoustics in Blake Hall, a depressing, cheaply built cement-cell type edifice, worsened Erlich's diction. But his views were plain as he nodded in agreement when Ernest Mandel said, "The student revolt can become the vanguard of the working class."

"HARD HATS" REFUTE RED THEORY

That is standard Marxist theory. But it might not prove to be the case. In New York City, May 7 and 8, 1970, workers in the Building & Construction Trades Union — the "hard hats" gave that Marxist theory a jolt felt round the world, when they clambered down from scaffoldings to rout a rabble of student detonators and professional agitators who had thrust a Red Flag into the arm of the statue of George Washington at Federal Hall in Wall Street. It was historically ironic and highly symbolic that Wall Street should have been the site of the rout, for Communists and Marxists use the name "Wall Street" as a class-struggle term signifying alleged capitalist exploitation of workers.

At the Fourth Annual Conference of Socialist Scholars in September 1968, it became plain that phase one of the radical Marxist operations in the United States had been successfully completed, and the teachers of destruction were ready to embark on phase two, a much more disciplined and sophisticated phase slated to be meshed closely with the international Marxist-Leninist apparatus of which Maoism is an offshoot.

Phase one in our country culminated in the March on the Pentagon, October 1967; the rebellion at Columbia University, April 1968; "the abdication" of President Johnson, March 1968; and the violent demonstrations during the 1968 Democratic National Convention in Chicago.

"REPRESSION" PROPAGANDA AS COVER-UP

In the final paragraphs of an article about the Socialist Scholars Conference at Rutgers, I wrote two months before the 1968 presidential elections:

"The between-sessions and corridor conversation at the Socialist Scholars Conference this month revealed that most of the participants and their youthful adherents, 'the detonators,' believe they can continue operations unharassed if Hubert H. Humphrey is elected in November, but will be 'repressed'—to use the Socialists' term—if Richard M. Nixon wins.

"Whoever wins, the Socialist Scholars intend to continue their Marxist-Leninist revolutionary struggle at home and abroad, acting as a fuse to human detonators to set off social explosions."

Now in 1970, the Marxist teachers of destruction and radical New Politics leaders are acting as fuses of detonators to set off social explosions, and are accusing the Nixon Administration of "repression," a baseless accusation formulated by the Socialist Scholars and their youthful pupils even before President Nixon was elected.

The effect of their propaganda may be seen in the following question asked of Dr. James Cheek, president of Howard University, by reporter Carl T. Rowan on the CBS television program "Face the Nation," August 2, 1970: "Dr. Cheek, you were quoted as saying in June that the Administration has turned from support of democratic principles to efforts of repression and oppression. Do you believe that still continues and on what do you base it?"

Dr. Cheek replied that he hadn't said that. "That's what the press stated I said." He went on to say that his position was that the Administration had not abandoned democratic principles, but that there had been things said by leaders in the Administration "that I think give rise to the impression of repression as well as oppression."

To create an impression of repression, without there being any actual repression, is what the radicals and New Politics leaders in our nation are trying to achieve in the effort to shield themselves from stringent criticism of, and any legal action against, their revolutionary, destructive and subversive activities.

CHAPTER 12

CAMPUS TROUBLES SPARKED

...By Teachers of Destruction

WHAT WAS RESPONSIBLE for the explosive situation on our campuses that culminated in the April 1970 shootings at Kent State University in Ohio?

Was the generally explosive situation on campuses caused by radical students acting spontaneously on their own initiative, or was it sparked primarily by advocacy of violent revolution on the part of Marxists such as Ernest Mandel, foreign "guest of honor" at the Socialist Scholars Conference at Rutgers in 1968, who proclaimed there that students are "the detonators" for triggering off social explosions creating a revolutionary situation, and then went on a two-months, coast-to-coast tour of more than thirty of our campuses to urge students to become detonators?

In our country, since 1952, far-fetched, tortured and exaggerated interpretations of the First and Fifth Amendments to our Constitution have progressively robbed our society and its institutions of proper protection from Marxist radicals inimical to the basic principles of our form of government. These judical interpretations, or misinterpretations, have given anarchists, violent revolutionaries, and criminals unlimited license for the most extreme kinds of advocacy and action.

Regarding our security, the Warren Court drew such a hair-splitting distinction between advocacy and action that it became almost impossible legally to restrain criminal advocacy until after the precise instant when it had been transformed into criminal action.

I myself have sat among Marxist radicals — young, middle-aged, and old — and listened to their open proclamation about this or that building or institution or community that they intended to "blow up" or "burn down."

It seems that under existing decisions of the Supreme Court, absolutely nothing can be done to restrain prospective arsonists and bombers from their advocacy and planning until they themselves or their pupils go forth and commit arson and bombing.

CRIMINAL LITERATURE

A specific case in point is the pamphlet "High School Reform: Towards a Student Movement" by Mark Kleiman of Students for a Democratic Society (SDS), a pamphlet that seeks to justify two specific crimes: the setting of trash can fires and the ringing of false fire alarms in schools.

Four years ago, hundreds of copies of the SDS high school pamphlet were distributed at the Socialist Scholars Conference; thousands upon thousands of that pamphlet have been distributed since then.

As soon as I first read it, I took it to the Fire Marshal at City Hall in New York City and also drew it to the attention of the Fire Underwriters Protective Association. In an article and newspaper column, I warned of the tragedies that could ensue from such SDS advocacy of school arson and demanded to know why the U.S. Post Office Department permits such criminal literature to be sent through the mails. Police and fire department officials in every state wrote to me about my article and column; so did leading insurance company executives.

What happened?

Nothing.

There is no legal way, it seems, to forbid or prevent distribution and mailing of the SDS pamphlet "High School Reform: Towards a Student Movement." Meantime, arson in schools and the setting off in schools of false fire alarms have cost millions upon millions of dollars and countless lives.

This year, in Brooklyn, New York, a mother and five children were burned to death in a residential fire that the Fire Department said could easily have been put out if nearby fire-fighting equipment had been available. But it wasn't. Why? It was at a neighborhood school in response to a deliberately set false fire alarm.

In July 1970, a $14,000,000 high school in Long Island was totally destroyed by fire and was officially declared to be a case of arson, with the fire set in a "social studies" classroom!

There will come a time, I am certain, when SDS instruction of high school students in arson and setting off false fire alarms will be halted. One day a high school will go up in flames as a result of arson and several hundred children and teachers will be burned or trampled to death.

Then — I predict — there will be legal recognition by the Supreme Court of the inherently dynamic relationship between advocacy and action, a recognition that advocacy is not a static, unproductive intellectual process but a clearly moving and causal one.

MARXISTS CONFUSE ISSUE

Nobody recognizes that truth more clearly than the Marxist teachers of destruction. Therefore they have waged in our country a brilliantly successful propaganda campaign to persuade Americans that *any* restriction of advocacy is a violation of our First Amendment.

Deliberately playing on the American people's revulsion against Hitlerism and their sacred belief in a person's innocence until proved guilty, the Marxist revolutionary radicals merged the ghosts of two dead men — Adolf Hitler and Joseph R. McCarthy — into one single giant specter depicted as hovering permanently over every nook and cranny of our land.

The propaganda campaign has been so shrewdly, persistently and militantly conducted that today many decent, law-abiding, loyal, educated and cultivated men and women in every field of endeavor are brainwashed into believing that any attempt to draw a distinction between liberty and license in our nation is "repressive."

The total intellectual acceptance today of the concept that *any* restraint on advocacy of any cause, notion, fad or act of criminality is *per se* fascistic or censorial has led to outrageous extremes and absurd anomalies. For example, the 1,750 daily newspapers in our country abide by a voluntary decency code adopted by the American Society of Newspaper Editors, yet many of these newspapers oppose editorially any restraint of absolute license — "freedom" they call it — of the campus and "underground" press. Evidently, today, all odious concepts are regarded as protected by the First Amendment, including murder — "Kill the pigs!"; arson — "Burn, baby, burn!"; violent insurrection and civil war — "guerrilla action."

I repeat: What was responsible for the explosive campus situation that culminated in the shootings at Kent State University in Ohio? Was it the action of students and National Guardsmen, or was it the kind of advocacy — to which I have listened for years and years — which is typified by the statements of an Ernest Mandel who proclaims, "Students are the detonators in the formula for triggering off a social explosion creating a revolutionary situation."? What kind of action does Mandel's advocacy lead to when he tells his fellow agitators, "As a revolutionary Marxist you must know that you cannot destroy capitalism piecemeal. You can abolish the structure only by overthrowing it, not by reforming it."?

LAWSUIT OVER ALIEN REVOLUTIONARY

Yet Ernest Mandel is today the central figure in a lawsuit brought against the United States government, a legal action striking at the very foundations of our nation as a sovereign host empowered to admit or bar entry of a foreign visitor.

Late in 1969, the Socialist Scholars again invited him to be their guest speaker, this time at Town Hall in Manhattan. The Justice Department barred Mandel from entry into our country by refusing to exempt him from legal provisions of the Immigration and Nationality Act of 1952, which proscribes admission to the United States of foreigners

Prof. Robert R. Bordhers stands in the rubble that was once his physics laboratory at Sterling Hall on the University of Wisconsin campus on 9/4/70. The building was destroyed on 8/24/70 by a bomb blast. Bordhers warned of a possible exodus of scholars from UW because of campus violence.   UPI belonging to a list of subversive organizations compiled by our Justice Department. It alone has authority to grant exemptions from a ban, and it was previously lifted in Mandel's case during the Kennedy and Johnson Administrations before his 1968 tour of our universities, at which time Ernest Mandel violated provisions of his visitor's visa.

Concerning the banning of Mandel, the *New York Times* reported, November 27, 1969: "Liberal academic figures in the United States have warned that the Mandel case raises the question of whether a person should be excluded from the United States because of his political views."

Immediately, the Socialist Scholars and their associates, including Princeton University Professor Arno Mayer, held a press conference to protest the action of our Justice Department.

The *New York Times* further reported:

"Miss Edith Tiger of the National Emergency Civil Liberties Committee said that Leonard Boudin, its counsel, was studying the matter to see if American participants in the events in which Dr. Mandel was to have taken part might challenge the constitutionality of the law that prevents them from hearing him."

Thus it became plain that once again pro-Communists are going to try to strike down yet another provision of our internal security laws. The story in the *New York Times* did not inform readers that the National Emergency Civil Liberties Committee was cited in Congress as "a Communist front," nor did *The Times* mention that Mandel was banned from France in 1968 following his instigation there of the May-June rebellion, an act of foreign intervention in that country's internal affairs, since Mandel is Belgian.

On October 28, 1969, the *New York Times* declared editorially that the Justice Department's banning of Mandel was "a senseless violation" of our First Amendment and also "idiotic." Again on March 26, 1970, the *New York Times* devoted an editorial to the Mandel case and declared that the Justice Department's action was a "vestige of the restrictive nineteen-fifties era" which strikes particularly "at teachers and writers for advocacy of and affiliation with leftwing causes." The newspaper went on to report, "Now a group of professors from six American institutions has called upon the Attorney General in Federal District Court to give the reasons why Dr. Mandel cannot be admitted for lectures and debates this spring or fall."

Again some essential facts were omitted.

All six litigating professors — David Marmelstein of Brooklyn Polytechnic Institute, Wassily Leontief of Harvard, Norman Birnbaum of Amherst, Robert L. Heilbroner of the New School for Social Research, Robert P. Wolff of Columbia, and Louis Menasche of Brooklyn Polytechnic — are Socialist Scholars.

I myself attended the Socialist Scholars Conferences for five years, 1965-1969, and no exponent of dissent from socialism and Marxism ever took part in the official program as a guest speaker or panelist. All debates are discussion of one side — the socialist side; there never was a pro-capitalist critique of socialism or any discussion of any constructive capitalist accomplishment in our society.

In addition to the *New York Times* and Socialist Scholars, three prominent academic figures—President Robert F. Goheen of Princeton, President Alan Simpson of Vassar and President J.E. Wallace Sterling of Stanford—are backing the admission of Ernest Mandel to our country and have issued public statements critical of our Justice Department in his case. Yet not one of the three distinguished university presidents was present at the Socialist Scholars Conference at Rutgers in 1968 when Mandel publicly urged students to be "detonators." Nor was one of the three present at Town Hall in 1969 to hear Mandel urge—via a recorded speech in English—the total destruction, not reform, of our governmental and social structure.

On March 30, 1970, the *New York Times* reported:

"Six American scholars brought suit in Federal Court in Brooklyn yesterday to restrain Secretary of State William P. Rogers and Attorney General John N. Mitchell from barring a Belgian Marxist from visiting the United States. . . .

"The scholars contended there was no evidence that he would engage in 'unlawful speech or conduct' and that he had been denied equal protection of the law and 'due process' ".

On December 2, 1969, *The Washington Post* carried a column by Frank Mankiewicz and Tom Braden that scathingly attacked Attorney General Mitchell and expressed the hope that he would "eventually be overruled in the Mandel case."

It is too bad that university presidents Goheen, Sterling and Simpson, and executives of *The Times* and *Washington Post* were not present at the "Tom Paine Awards" dinner given by the National Emergency Civil Liberties Committee at the Hotel Americana in New York City, December 12, 1969, an affair at which Leonard Boudin, counsel of the NECLC and attorney for the Socialist Scholars in the Ernest Mandel case, recited the history of his victories in cases subsidized by the NECLC that went to the Supreme Court. Mr. Boudin declared it had not been necessary to go to court in other cases supported by the Committee "because the Government surrendered." Then he appealed for funds to fight the Mandel case.

During the fund-raising, Boudin proudly introduced to the more than 1,300 people present his daughter, Kathy Boudin.

ADVOCACY BECOMES ACTION

Had prominent university presidents and columnists and eminent newspaper publishers been present at the NECLC dinner, they would better understand, perhaps, how the guest speakers' "advocacy" is quickly translated into the kind of "action" which, in Detroit, August 1970, led to a Federal Grand Jury indictment of Kathy Boudin "for conspiring to bomb business and educational buildings throughout the country" and — as the *New York Times* paraphrased the indictment — "to kill and injure those inside."

Only three months after her appearance with her father at the dinner in the Americana Hotel given by the Communist-front National Emergency Civil Liberties Committee which is helping to subsidize the Ernest Mandel case, Kathy Boudin made front-page headlines as one of the two young women alleged to have fled the SDS Weatherman bomb factory in the house on West 11th Street in Manhattan, which was wrecked by explosions that took the life of SDS member Ted Gold and that of at least two other SDS members.

It seems that those young people who heeded Mandel's "detonator" advocacy moved promptly and dynamically into action.

Moreover, at the NECLC dinner, December 12, 1969, Conor Cruise O'Brien, formerly of the New York University faculty and recently elected member of the Republic of Ireland Parliament, showed the guests a new pamphlet put out by the SDS Weatherman faction, called on everyone present to study it, and declared, "Violence is the only way to assure moderation."

All this was in the presence of Leonard Boudin, attorney-at-law, who was well aware, when he proudly presented his daughter Kathy to the audience, that she had been arrested in Chicago during the 1968 Democratic National Convention on charges of loosing a "stink bomb" in the lobby of Palmer House, and had been arrested again in Chicago, October 2, 1969, on charges of "aggravated battery" against police officers. Also, Kathy Boudin had been an applicant for copyright of *The Bust Book,* a paperback written for "political prisoners" which states that "the cop and the judge wear different uniforms, but they both serve the same system we seek to destroy."

NEWS MEDIA FAIL TO REPORT PLOTTING

At the Hotel Americana ballroom, attorney-at-law Leonard Boudin and his daughter Kathy took part in and applauded proceedings which I described in a newspaper column written not only to inform the public but also as a kind of desperate plea to my press colleagues and therefore entitled "What Is New York City News?" It was datelined New York City, December 15, 1969. Here is the text:

"What is New York City news? Sometimes, though my home is in Manhattan and following the news is my profession, I wonder. Are subjects of front-page stories in New York City newspapers news? Are individuals appearing on prime TV New York news time news? Specifically, are David Dellinger, Dr. 'Captain' Howard Levy and Harlem Black Panther Tom Jolly news?

"Each of them has figured prominently in newspapers and on TV news during the last ten days. Yet nobody but me in the entire New York City above-ground, non-radical press was present in the Hotel Americana Imperial Ballroom, December 12, 1969, to hear them speak at the 'Tom Paine Awards' dinner held by the Communist-front National Emergency Civil Liberties Committee (NECLC).

"David Dellinger, leader of Mobilization for Peace and one of the eight original defendants on trial in Chicago for conspiracy to riot at the 1968 Democratic National Convention, is in the New York City papers almost every day. Dr. 'Captain' Howard Levy, former Army medical officer who spent 26 months in prison for refusing to obey military orders, was featured recently in the *New York Post.* Harlem Black Panther Tom Jolly spoke his piece on all New York City TV channels immediately after the Los Angeles shoot-out with Panthers and the shooting of Panther leader Fred Hampton in Chicago. On TV, Jolly charged 'genocide' and 'fascist murder' of Panthers by 'the Nixon regime and imperialist United States.'

"But on Friday night, December 12, no TV or newspaper reporter was in the Americana ballroom, where more than 1,300 people paid $17.50 per ticket to dine on lobster bisque, filet mignon, and *bombe glacée jubilée,* to cover presentation of NECLC awards to David Dellinger, Dr. Howard Levy, and TV star Tom Smothers (for whom a stand-in accepted the award and read a message). Nobody in the press was there to hear NECLC Chairman Corliss Lamont of Columbia University philosophy department call on 'surprise speaker' Black Panther Tom Jolly, who feasted on goodies while two Panther guards sat beside him. . . .

"First speaker was Conor Cruise O'Brien. . .who analyzed the new pamphlet put out by Weatherman, violent SDS faction in our country, and called on everybody present to study it. 'Violence,' declared O'Brien, 'is the only way to assure moderation.'

Northern Illinois University students in De Kalb watch as an overturned Illinois State car burns on campus early 5/20/70. Car and three other vehicles were set afire by some 500 students who went on a rampage for the second straight night. Thirty-one persons were arrested. Three policemen and three demonstrators were slightly injured.   UPI

"Next came fund-raiser Marxist economist Douglas Dowd, professor at Cornell University. Exclusive of pledges and cash dropped in baskets passed around the dinner tables, more than $32,000 in contributions was collected. Dr. Lamont gave $6,000, Stewart Mott, Park Avenue millionaire, new member of the NECLC national council, and honored guest on the dais, gave $700.

"Next, 'Captain' Howard Levy delivered a harangue which culminated with the cry, 'F--- the Army!' He called on the audience to chant the slogan. 'F--- the Army!' he screamed and hundreds of diners responded 'F--- the Army!' Levy was not satisfied. 'Louder!' he commanded. 'F--- the Army!' they shouted obediently. 'Louder!' yelled Levy. 'F--- the Army!' screamed the crowd. 'Good!' said Levy triumphantly, and declared, 'Nixon has an obsession not to be the first American President to lose a war. He doesn't know it, but he's going to be the first American President to lose the Army!'

"Black Panther Tom Jolly was invited to the dais microphone. 'All power to the people!' he cried, and did his vile thing, blackening the name of everything decent, honorable and legal in our nation.

"Then came the vilest of all — David Dellinger. He repeated every obscenity yelled in the Chicago courtroom by Black Panther Bobby Seale before he was sentenced to four years in jail for contempt of court, and then said, 'Bobby is a beautiful person.' Dellinger said, 'We defendants had been in daily intimate contact with Fred Hampton, right up until he was murdered in Chicago. He was a beautiful person. He was murdered in cold blood by the Chicago pigs and Nixon Administration. Fred Hampton met with us daily to discuss not only the trial but also other actions and tactics.'

"Where were the New York City newspaper and TV reporters? I don't know. But I do know that those on the NECLC dinner dais in the Hotel Americana ballroom constitute a kind of board-of-directors for violent revolution in our nation. They seem to enjoy privileged sanctuary from the press. Why? I can't figure it out. At any rate, I can report that the speakers at the NECLC dinner expect the revolution to take place 'one year from now.' They are drunk with success and couldn't care less about what the Kremlin says, because they figure they are destined to be the world leaders of the Communist revolution that will overthrow the United

States Government and take charge internationally in the liquidation of capitalism and of the Free World's freedom."

Within less than a year after the dinner held by pro-Communists and Marxist teachers of destruction at the Americana Hotel in December 1969, social explosions set off by students and professional agitators acting as "detonators" rocked the nation — at Santa Barbara, California, in the house on West 11th Street and the bombings of buildings in New York City; in the shootings at Kent State University in Ohio and at Jackson State College in Mississippi.

FALSE ARGUMENT FOR RETAINING TEACHERS OF DESTRUCTION

Yet many of the most prominent leaders in our country— academic, legal and governmental — continue to draw a hair-splitting distinction between "advocacy" and "action," and continue to maintain in the name of "academic freedom" and "freedom of speech" under our First Amendment the utter fiction that dedicated Communists and Marxist radicals are willing and able to occupy teaching positions on faculties without "bringing politics into the classroom" and without mingling their on and off campus activities.

Concerning this fiction, the *Santa Monica Evening Outlook* asked editorially about the case of Angela Davis (self-proclaimed Communist, Black Panther, and pupil of Socialist Scholar Herbert Marcuse), who was barred from continued employment as a teacher in the University of California at Los Angeles philosophy department, "Is Miss Davis Two People?" The editorial continued, "We would ask the academic freedom buffs who are rising in defense of Miss Angela Davis, 'Is she human like the rest of us, or is she really two people?' " The newspaper then answered its own rhetorical question: "She is human. She can't be two people — one non-political and the other highly political."

At the very first annual conference of the Socialist Scholars in 1965, Dr. Eugene Genovese, who won his notorious fight to remain on the faculty of Rutgers

University as two people — an on-campus Genovese and an off-campus Genovese — acknowledged and cynically proclaimed among his own Marxist group that he was not and could not be two people, when he said, "The political separation — activist and academician — is a matter of convenience. *That we all know.*"

For Marxist teachers of destruction, the alleged political separation between academician and activist is purely a matter of their own convenience (and our inconvenience!), as Angela Davis and Ernest Mandel and Leonard Boudin and his associates all know.

Apparently, the people who do not know it, or refuse to acknowledge it, are most of the academicians, sociologists and civic leaders on Presidential commissions of inquiry into the causes of campus unrest and violence, and also those prominent men and women who are supporting the absurd allegation that an agitator such as Ernest Mandel can be two people, of whom one can be admitted into the United States as a guest without his being accompanied by the other.

In my view, very little that is constructive can be done about campus unrest and violence in our nation until the academic and legal communities acknowledge the fact that ideas have consequences, and that advocacy is *per se* dynamic, not peacefully reflective or passively contemplative.

YOUNG REVOLUTIONARIES

...They were Taught that Way

OPENLY PROUD OF their rapid progress toward destruction of our American way of life, the Socialist Scholars—Marxist revolutionary brain trust in our country— gathered together at Hofstra University, Hempstead, New York, September 5-7, 1969, to hold a Fifth Annual Conference.

Even if television cameras had been grinding and wire service reporters had been taking notes at the conference panel discussions, which they were not, no Socialist Scholar would have minced words about his real revolutionary role in "the movement".

The members know they have no effectively organized anti-socialist or anti-revolutionary opposition in our country today. They knew in 1965, when they formed the SSC, that they had successfully used the slogans of "McCarthyism" and "Red-baiting" and "witch-hunt" to disarm their intellectual foes; the Socialist Scholars knew too that the U.S. Department of Justice had been disarmed legally by a series of decisions favorable to Communists handed down by the Warren Court's interpretation of the First and Fifth Amendments to our Constitution.

The Socialist Scholars were then certain, as they had been during the last five years, that almost nobody among the bewildered majority of Americans asking "How do they get that way?" about violent young revolutionaries in the United States, France, Japan, Mexico and other countries, would come up with the only correct answer: "Because they were taught that way."

Take Socialist Scholar Martin Jay, for example, a Teaching Fellow in Social Science, School of General Education, Harvard University. He told a large audience of Socialist Scholars and radical students in the Multipurpose Room, Student Center, Hofstra University, "Our movement is a movement which, in effect, is a total break with America."

THE INFLUENCE OF ONE PROFESSOR

The topic of the SSC panel discussion in which Martin Jay took part was "Marcuse [Herbert]: His Works and Influence." The other panelists were Ronald Aronson, Assistant Professor of Humanistic Studies, Wayne State University; Paul Breines, University of Wisconsin; and Stanley Aronowitz, columnist for the radical news-weekly *Guardian.*

The very long paper presented by Ronald Aronson was in the form of an open letter headed "Dear Herbert." It shows precisely why Prof. Herbert Marcuse of the University of California at San Diego, author of *One Dimensional Man* and *Eros and Civilization,* is the internationally recognized intellectual mentor of "Red" Danny Cohn-Bendit, who played a key role in the 1968 May-June rebellion in France, and of "Red" Rudi Dutschke in West Berlin. Ronald Aronson's paper shows too, in a most vivid, personal way, why and how Marcuse, an Old Leftist, has become the intellectual idol of the so-called New Left in influencing youths toward anarchism and hedonism.

Ronald Aronson wrote:

"Dear Herbert:

". . . I want to begin by emphasizing that for myself and a few friends, studying with you was one of the decisive experiences of our lives. Your thought, personality, style of teaching and writings were overpowering. . . . you helped us to take our stand in Western thought and still be Marxists . . . You introduced us to a perspective which was new and revolutionary, which made sense of our lives and helped us find our way as radicals. . . .

"You were never humble, and for that I thank you. . . . No wonder we felt dominated by you. No wonder we argued after every class about what you meant, read and discussed your books as soon as they came out, quoted you against each other, made 'What would Marcuse think?' our major intellectual principle. . . ."

Any non-Marxist who is appalled at or mystified by the anarchism and violence of revolutionary youth in our country and abroad, need only read Ronald Aronson's own account of his own life in the paper "Dear Herbert" to gain full understanding. Rhetorically, Aronson asks how it is possible for him to be himself "and live in America." Answering himself, he writes, "The only answer that makes sense to me is this: creating my identity *and* becoming political. Being myself *and* in opposition. Seeing revolution as the way to liberate us all to live a life that is truly our own." He continues: "What a leap I just took! A whole account of a life-search which doesn't once mention politics, and suddenly I proclaim the necessity for revolution."

He then calls on scholars to write a study—written "as Marx did" — to show "that fully-developed capitalism is necessarily totalitarian. . . . I mean that the corporations' pursuit of profits through the mass production and sale of commodities has spread to every geographic area, every inch of land, every population subgroup, every activity, every hour of the day."

HOW YOUTHS BECOME ANARCHISTS

Do American university presidents, corporation heads, government leaders and communications media executives really want to know how middle-class American youths become violent anarchists wanting to bring down the system?

It is not possible to find an explanation more specific than that given in the following verbatim quotation from Professor Ronald Aronson's paper: ". . . Only the sense of a wholly new way of life will do, the demand to be radical—myself—in working, in loving, in thinking, in feeling, in eating, in joking. Anything which separates me from myself oppresses, whether it comes from America or its radical opposition. Not only Nixon's patriotism oppresses, but also the idea of any community over the individuals. Not only bourgeois morality, but any morality which imposes thoughts from the outside. Not only the idea of self-sacrifice for a class society, but any kind of self-sacrifice for a cause beyond me. Not only the middle class postponement of pleasure, but any postponement of pleasure, coming from any source. Not only guilt about not fighting for my homeland, but also guilt of any sort, even towards black people. Not only middle class role playing is outrageous—but any kind of role playing, even the role of radical intellectual or heavy politico. I have become a revolutionary because America, while willing to sell me everything, won't let me be myself. Should I give up this or that part of myself to oppose America?

"Do you see now? It's not politics that are at stake, or my ideas. My whole being is at stake. To reclaim a part of it I have to reclaim it all—otherwise I'm just playing the game. I don't have the feeling of America slowly closing in on me, the need to retreat to some small corner in order to keep mankind's hopes alive. Even 'mankind' is just another oppressive phrase to me; just another abstraction threatening to suffocate *me*. My experience is of being lost in the Smiling sick sea and of need to Wrench myself out step by step; my need is to avoid and destroy all of Their categories in my life, to reject bull---- in all of its disguises, to let America have none of myself, to get whole, and to become a guerrilla."

Doubtless students studying with Socialist Scholars will be given a classroom assignment to study Ronald Aronson's maxim that "revolutionaries need to engage the whole person: his activity, his imagination, his sense of lost hopes. Not tracing the structure of capitalism, but blowing people's minds."

That's what the Socialist Scholars are all about—blowing people's minds, and especially young people's minds. At SSC panel sessions, the devastating path of the intellectual hurricane blowing thousands of young American victims into a mindless culture of drugs, obscenity, pornography and anarchy was as discernible as the weather map path of a hurricane.

At a panel session on "The Student Response to the American Century," James O'Brien of the University of Wisconsin traced the historic development of American socialism in this century, praising all socialists, regardless of faction, for the role they played in trying to destroy capitalism, from Walter Lippmann of the Intercollegiate Socialist Society (Harvard, 1913) to Mark Rudd of Students for a Democratic Society (Columbia, 1968); from John Dewey, author of "progressive education" to Herbert Aptheker of the present Communist Party, U.S.A. and Institute for Marxist Studies; from the late Norman Thomas, of the Socialist Party and Social Democratic Federation, to Michael Harrington, author of *The Other America*, a present leader of Americans for Democratic Action and chairman of the League for Industrial Democracy.

INFLUENCE OF JOHN DEWEY, SOCIALIST

Few analysts among the post-World War II generation are aware that American philosopher John Dewey, father of our twentieth century "progressive education" system, was a dedicated socialist and long-time president of the League for Industrial Democracy (originally the Intercollegiate Socialist Society).

Dewey's influence shifted American education away from its traditional aim of individual achievement and success to the aim of collective "social purpose." Dewey charged that education for individual success was "the deliberate act of a capitalist class bent on securing its own supremacy." He advocated "controlling methods of teaching and discipline and materials of study" in order to create "education for a new social order"—meaning socialism.

Neither John Dewey nor any other socialist has been able, however, to construct or even depict a free and workable society without the incentives to individual success.

On October 20, 1949, when the League for Industrial Democracy celebrated Dewey's ninetieth birthday, Joy Elmer

Morgan, editor of the National Education Association *Journal*, congratulated Dewey on behalf of the NEA's 400,000 members and on behalf of the "30,000,000 children in America whose living will be so different because of the teaching of John Dewey."

Their lives did become different, so much different that now, only a single generation later, the sad effects are upon us and the entire American educational system is in danger of breaking down. Due to Dewey's program of trying to teach the child to be part of the whole community as soon as he or she enters first grade, Johnny and Mary not only can't read or spell and lack a sense of the need for self-development and self-control, but also have lost respect for authority. Mostly due to Dewey, millions of American school children have been forced to waste hours and hours of the school week on imprecise social studies instead of devoting their precious youth-time, attention and energy to precise learning of reading, writing, arithmetic, history and geography. In consequence, hordes of American children reach high school and even college without the basic skills required for living in the real, not Utopian, world, and for earning a living by their own efforts instead of living on welfare and unemployment benefits subsidized by others' efforts.

In November 1970, the Economic Development Council of New York City reported that the current heavy migration of business firms out of the city is mainly owing to the city's public schools "which are not graduating young people who can read and write." The Council declared that at least 10,000 clerical jobs in the city are going begging because businesses cannot find competent young people to fill them.

In 1949, John Dewey wrote "Education and the Social Order" in which he demanded abolition of authoritarian management of schools, and called for high school and college students' active participation in the larger community life "in a new type of citizenship in which political questions will be seen in their economic background and bearings."

Though Dewey shied away from identifying himself as a Marxian pragmatist, his 1949 pamphlet was based on Marxist economic determinism. He declared that if only students could be taught in the way he proposed, they would be ready to take their own active part in "aggressive participation in bringing about a new social order."

That "aggressive participation" is now upon us, in the form of SDS "participatory democracy" and in other aggressive forms of collective socialist action.

As a result, our nation is plunged into an educational crisis recognized by almost all our citizens, including such a long-time advocate of Deweyism as liberal socialist Dr. Sidney Hook of New York University.

At the Socialist Scholars Conference in September 1969, as James O'Brien of Wisconsin University was discussing his paper, "The Student Response to the American Century," and was tracing the history of American socialism in our century from Walter Lippmann and John Dewey to the late Norman Thomas of the Socialist Party, O'Brien boasted, "Capitalism is in its death period, and some progressive capitalists acknowledge it."

SOME CAPITALISTS ALSO BACKED HITLER

Indeed some do, even as some wealthy German, French and British capitalists, Catholic, Protestant and Jewish, backed National Socialist Adolf Hitler during the early 1930's, hoping to ride on the crest of "the wave of the future."

In our country today, there are many "progressive capitalists" financing socialist attacks on our great corporations, the furnishers of essential services and the producers of consumer goods—from ethical pharmaceutical drugs to insecticides, from automobiles to transistors, from computers to television sets and toys.

It is true that no human institution is faultless, and our great business corporations are not; but muckraking against American business always has been a socialist business, and from it sprang the current fad for "consumerism" which had its origin in the Communist-organized subversive Consumer's Union founded in 1935. It remained under Communist control until 1953, when changes in personnel were made and the organization was removed from the House Committee on Internal Security list of subversive organizations. There is no question that the American consumer needs legal protection against fraud, injury, unfair business practices and other criminal activities. But there is also no question that there exists in our nation today a deliberate campaign of vilification against American corporate enterprise by socialists, and especially by Socialist Scholars.

The American business corporation was the main target of the Fifth Annual Socialist Scholars Conference at Hofstra University, and the conferees linked the radical student movement closely with the anti-corporation campaign. All Marxist-Leninists believe, "The theory of the weakest link is the theory of the decisive link." At the panel on "The Student Response to the American Century," Bruce Brown of Washington University said, "The university is the weak link of capital corporate structure." Brown explained that the corporation is the "nuclear institution" around which American capitalism is organized, and he charged that in the United States "affluence is only attained through the surrender of control to corporate bureaucracy." Describing himself as a "revolutionary," Bruce Brown told the Socialist Scholars, "We must begin an anti-corporate struggle on its own terrain and not wait for a crisis." He went on to say that the term "youth" should be used to define "a group only in part defined by age, that is, a modality of society free of bureaucratic [capitalist] control."

Bruce Brown's statement explains the seeming paradox in a "New Left" American radicalism that professes rejection of "anyone over 30" but takes direction from Old Leftist septuagenarian Herbert Marcuse and from middle-aged Herbert Aptheker of the Communist Party, U.S.A.

To make sure of not being misunderstood, Bruce Brown explained, "The student movement is the catalyst for extending revolution outside the campuses."

What the Socialist Scholars mean by saying they will introduce into the classroom teaching materials written from "an explicitly socialist perspective" was made clear in Bruce Brown's remarks. This "scholar" declared, "Marxism is the only theory of capitalistic development; to deny Marxism is to deny that capitalism still exists."

It won't exist very much longer in the United States, and neither will the American corporation, if the Socialist Scholars have their way.

On Saturday, September 6, 1969, the guest of honor at the Fifth Annual Conference of Socialist Scholars, Robin Blackburn, British editor of the influential *New Left Review*, spoke at length in a panel session on "Recent European Theory and the American Left."

OVERTHROW OF OUR MORALS AND CULTURE

Mr. Blackburn explained, "Lenin is not difficult to accept by us Western revolutionaries." It is a mistake, he said, to allege that Lenin taught the necessity of one single revolutionary party. At certain stages of development— Blackburn said—Lenin favored the expediency "of a number of competing revolutionary groups." Blackburn continued, "If the revolution is a complex totality, so must be the revolutionary party." He called for overthrow of "the hegemony of bourgeois culture and creation of a genuinely revolutionary counter-culture." There must be a decisive break with middle-class (bourgeois) culture, he said, a break that is "the reverse of Puritanism." He said such a socialist culture "is impossible to achieve without the violent overthrow of the capitalist regime."

As I said earlier, the Socialist Scholars no longer mince words.

However, even Blackburn's call for "violent overthrow" was not explicitly socialist enough to suit him and his listeners, and so he went into great detail, putting current affairs in such clear perspective that there is no longer the slightest necessity for continued discussion in general academic, governmental or law enforcement circles about the significance of the "youth movement" and its role in our nation's affairs, now, during the Vietnam War, or later, after it has come to an end.

"Youth culture," said Robin Blackburn, "takes out a segment of society from bourgeois society." He praised the hippies and yippies and all manner of freak-out youth, including the 300,000 at the 1969 Woodstock Festival in New York State. He praised highly the American "underground culture" because "its explicit themes are anticapitalist."

And so they are.

ANTI-CAPITALISM, OBSCENITY, DRUGS

There is not a single underground newspaper or magazine in the United States which does not carry anti-capitalist political propaganda along with the obscenity and pornography.

Though the United Nations World Health Organization has issued the strongest condemnation of marijuana as introduction to use of mind-blowing narcotics, there is scarcely a single Leftist in our country who does not oppose our laws against use and sale of marijuana.

At the Fifth Annual Conference of Socialist Scholars, I overheard two members—one from Fairleigh Dickinson in New Jersey and one from New York State University at Stonybrook—talk about the "outrageous pig-administration cooperation in marijuana repression" and go on to praise marijuana as a useful means of "liberating" students from "middle class authoritarianism."

The Socialist Scholars in Adams Hall at Hofstra University, September 6, 1969, loudly applauded Robin Blackburn's analysis of youth culture. But they gave still more enthusiastic approval to his analysis of current "anarcho-populism" in the advanced industrial nations. In the United States and elsewhere, he explained, anarcho-populism should be favorably regarded because it is undermining "the archaic institution of private property."

To foster anarcho-populism in our nation, the Socialist Scholars—aware of the multiracial, culturally diverse nature of our population—strongly favor a multiplicity of radical groups and organizations among us. Indeed, the Socialist Scholars are assiduously promoting as many radical groups as possible, believing that in our big country with its big and re-

The Sterling Hall Physics building on the University of Wisconsin campus which houses the Army Mathematics Research Center stands shattered on 8/24/70 after a bomb exploded inside the building. One person was killed by the explosion.   UPI

gionally diverse population, variety is not only the spice of Socialist life but also its bread and butter. The Socialist Scholars are far too smart to put all their eggs in one Party basket.

In the fall of 1969, for the fifth time in succession, I was all alone among members of the non-radical press in reporting on the annual conference of the Socialist Scholars. There is no mystery at all about their movement; it is what Martin Jay of Harvard University says it is—"a total break with America."

On campuses throughout our nation, Socialist Scholars are training our children to make that break. In virtually all our academic communities, Socialist Scholars are studying, researching and teaching the most effective means for violent overthrow of our government and destruction of our way of life.

Chapter 14

RESEARCHING CAPITALISM
TO DEATH

THERE IS INSUFFICIENT awareness in the general public mind, throughout our country, of the power and influence exerted by many faculty members at our colleges and universities.

The public's mental image of a scholar is a person mostly or even solely occupied with teaching, writing and doing research pertaining to his own scholarly discipline. The proverbial stereotype is of the absent-minded professor dwelling in an ivory tower, where he thinks deep thoughts in solitude or in company with a few fellow intellectuals far removed from the everyday or workaday world.

To defend academic freedom on campus, Americans talk about the "right to teach" and "right of inquiry" and "right to the free exchange of ideas"—all excellent and fruitful concepts within our basic traditions of freedom.

Since December 15, 1791, however, when our Bill of Rights was adopted, a great many internal and external conditions have dynamically affected our basic traditions. Our Founding Fathers sought in the eighteenth century to change and improve the traditions of man's historical past, not to obliterate them. They sought to free man and enlarge his horizons, not to free man by changing the nature of man. They did not and could not foresee that in the middle of the nineteenth century there would emerge into world prominence an ideologue, Karl Marx, who would seek to change the basic nature of man and who would preach and teach—as the Communist Manifesto declares—"the forcible overthrow of all existing social conditions."

Nor could our Founding Fathers foresee that suddenly in the twentieth century, after World War II, the United States would become the dominant power in the free world and would assume throughout it the heaviest possible political, economic, military and social responsibilities.

INFLUENCE FAR BEYOND CONFINES OF CAMPUS

This sudden mid-twentieth century change in the role of the United States greatly affected the role of faculty members at our institutions of higher learning. Since 1947, our nation has been operating a multitude of international aid programs and engaging in all manner of activities abroad that are subsidized by the Federal government or by tax-exempt foundations. Since 1957, when the Soviet Union sent Sputnik into space, we have embarked on a domestic program of multi-billion dollar aid to education with all kinds of taxpayer-subsidized fellowships, scholarships and university projects requiring grants-in-aid.

As a result, university professors enjoying power to recommend or deny recommendation to students and scholars seeking federal, state, private business or foundation financial help for a multiplicity of local, national and international endeavors now exercise tremendous influence at home and abroad. The power of a professor, or small group of professors, to deny recommendation to a student or researcher seeking a Fulbright or Woodrow Wilson fellowship, or a Ford or Carnegie Foundation grant, is power indeed. By giving high grades to favored students and channeling them into faculty-determined fields of favored research for the earning of a master's or doctor's degree, professors can and often do wield an influence extending far beyond the confines of the campus and even beyond the boundaries of our nation.

Aware of all this, the Socialist Scholars and their radical Marxist associates encouraged the Communist revolutionary Students for a Democratic Society to establish in June 1966 an important research group, the SDS Radical Education

Project (REP) with headquarters at Ann Arbor, Michigan, and also an affiliate, the North American Congress on Latin America (NACLA).

The main objective of REP—intimately related through sponsors and advisors to the leftist Institute for Policy Studies in Washington, D.C., and to the Fund for the Republic's Center for the Study of Democratic Institutions at Santa Barbara, California—is to research capitalism to death.

By early 1968, two vitally important documents had been widely distributed by the New Politics movement: an REP statement of purpose, and a NACLA research methodology guide.

The Radical Education Project document contains, among others, the following statements of policy and belief:

- "the great promise of American abundance is perverted and thwarted by the functioning of contemporary capitalism;"
- "America is held in political and moral stalemate not only by sheer economic and political force, but also by deadening ideology . . . celebrating the American Way of Life, the American Dream, the American Century;"
- "anti-communism is a central element in this ideological manipulation of belief . . .;"
- "Violent revolution is to be recognized and deplored for its high human cost; but . . . where the oppressed lack political power, violent overthrow may be the necessary, though not sufficient, precondition to economic and political freedom."

SPONSORS OF RADICAL PROJECT

In light of the events in our country since the 1968 Democratic National Convention, it is very interesting to study the partial list of original sponsors published by the SDS Radical Education Project. They are:

Ralph Andreano	David Dellinger
Philip Berrigan	Stanley Diamond
Julian Bond	Douglas Dowd
Robert Browne	Hal Draper
Richard Cloward	Barrows Dunham

Robert Engler
Jules Feiffer
W.H. Ferry
Phillip Foner
Norm Fruchter
William Gamson
Julien Gendell
John Gerassi
Ernest Goodman
Paul Goodman
Nat Hentoff
David Horowitz
Leo Huberman
Raghavan Iyer
Paul Jacobs
Julius Jacobson
Gabriel Kolko
Andrew Kopkind
William Kunstler
Paul Lauter
Richard Lichtman
Staughton Lynd
Herbert Marcuse
Seymour Melman

Jack Minnis
Barrington Moore
Charles Moskos
Charles E. Osgood
Linus Pauling
Victor Perlo
James A. Pike
Marc Pilisuk
Victor Rabinowitz
Anatol Rapoport
Marc Raskin
Kenneth Rexroth
Sumner M. Rosen
Richard Shaull
Sol Stern
Harvey Swados
Harold Taylor
Michael Walzer
Arthur Waskow
Harvey Wheeler
William A. Williams
Marshall Windmiller
Howard Zinn

Three of the foregoing REP sponsors became nationally known via television during the Chicago demonstrations: Julian Bond of Georgia; David Dellinger, a main revolutionist; and Staughton Lynd, formerly of Yale University.

Philip Berrigan is the priest now serving a penitentiary sentence for his part in pouring blood on and destroying Selective Service System files at Catonsville, Maryland.

BLACK BALLOT BOX PROGRAM

Robert Browne is a professor of economics at Fairleigh Dickinson University, New Jersey. He is founder and executive director of the Black Economic Research Center in Harlem, Manhattan, and is author of the article "Separation" in *Ebony* magazine, August 1970, in which he advocates:

"But a new, independent black nation carved out of North America may be too grand, too ambitious, too visionary a goal for most blacks. Many, perhaps most, black separatists feel that a satisfactory degree of black liberation is achievable with a lesser degree of separation than complete independence. Consequently, we have other models of separation to test. One of the most promising is that of black control of one or more of the existing state governments, acquired via the ballot box. . . .

"Such a state-wide political take-over, regardless of which state was involved, would presently require a substantial immigration of black population (no state now has higher than a 44 per cent black population) as well as a higher degree of black unity and black political involvement than we have yet seen. Nevertheless, such an achievement is not only within the realm of possibility, it offers far more promising benefits than do the projected black take-overs of a dozen major cities within the next decade. . . ."

OTHER SPONSORS OF REP

SDS Radical Education Project sponsor Richard Cloward is the Columbia University professor who, as heretofore set forth, is a Socialist Scholar and main author of the concept that the welfare system should be used as a means of bankrupting our government. He is a main ideological and activist founder of the National Welfare Rights Organization.

Professor Douglas Dowd of Cornell University is a Socialist Scholar and was a main supporter of the kind of radicalism that led to the guns-on-campus revolution there in 1969.

Jules Feiffer is the well-known cartoonist.

W.H. Ferry was in 1966 vice president of the Center for the Study of Democratic Institutions at Santa Barbara, and was the speaker at the Democratic Western States Conference in Seattle, August 6, 1962, who launched into such a vitriolic, untrue attack against the Federal Bureau of Investigation and its director, J. Edgar Hoover, that the then U.S. Attorney General, Robert F. Kennedy, publicly disavowed and apologized for Ferry's remarks. In that speech, W.H. Ferry referred boastfully to President Kennedy as "my former student." Immediately thereafter, I inquired about it at the White House and received the following official reply: "President Kennedy took an English course at the age of fourteen years at Choate School under Mr. W.H. Ferry and has not seen him since."

Other persons closely affiliated with the Center for the Study of Democratic Institutions at the time they sponsored the SDS Radical Education Project in 1966 were Dr. Linus Pauling, 1970 Lenin Peace Prize winner; the late radical Bishop James A. Pike (who was ousted from his church post); Harvey Wheeler; Raghavan N. Iyer; Paul Jacobs; and Richard Lichtman.

Andrew Kopkind is a former reporter for the left-liberal *New Republic* magazine who, in October 1968, founded the radical newsletter *Mayday*, later changed to *Hard Times*. He described the original title *Mayday* as follows, "The title is a triple pun that we hope will appeal to different constituencies. Mayday is the international distress signal, a call by radicals to the streets, and a reference to springtime for the counter-culture love generation." *Hard Times* is self-described in its promotional literature as "ammunition in an arsenal of guerrilla journalism."

Mr. Kopkind is a friend of the violent SDS Weatherman faction and was arrested in Chicago, October 1969, on charges of "disorderly conduct" during the Weatherman march through the Loop to demonstrate solidarity with the "Conspiracy Seven" group on trial there. He himself reported in the October 20-27, 1969 issue of *Hard Times:*

"There were twelve people in our two-man cell at the Chicago Police Headquarters last Saturday after the SDS 'Weatherman' march through the Loop. Our charges ran from disorderly conduct (my own) through possession of explosives to attempted murder. . . .

" 'Weatherman' demands the willing suspension of disbelief. As an ideology of communism and a strategy of revolution, it . . . asks that radicals become revolutionaries, completely collectivize their lives, and struggle to death if necessary. . . .

"Now some say that the police attacked first, and others say the weathermen took the offensive, but it is true that the weathermen did not shrink from the fight, and we all thought in the cell block that night that simply not to fear fighting is a kind of winning."

Ten months later, several of the principal leaders of "Weatherman" were indicted by a Federal Grand Jury in Detroit for conspiring to bomb buildings and to kill and injure people.

Immediately after *Mayday* (subsequently *Hard Times*) was launched in October 1968, the *New York Times* reported about the two-day-old journal:

"The first issue of *Mayday*, a four-page weekly tabloid oriented toward muckraking and radical politics, was published in Washington Friday under the editorship of three nationally known journalists.

"The editors are Andrew Kopkind, James Ridgeway, former reporters for the *New Republic*, and Robert Sherrill, correspondent for *The Nation* . . .

"Ralph Nader, lawyer and crusader for better consumer protection laws, is consulting editor . . ."

(Mr. Nader remained a consulting editor on the masthead of *Mayday* and then *Hard Times* until after I wrote the article " 'Raider' Or 'Guerrilla' — Will The Real Ralph Nader Please Stand Up?" for my own magazine and *Barron's*. Shortly thereafter, Mr. Nader's name disappeared from the *Hard Times* masthead.)

Another original sponsor of the SDS Radical Education Project was William Kunstler, notorious attorney for the Chicago Conspiracy Seven and for the vanished H. Rap Brown who is wanted for trial in Maryland on a charge of incitement to riot in the burnings, lootings and shootings in Cambridge, Md.

REP sponsors Herbert Marcuse and Seymour Melman are Socialist Scholars. Professor Melman is a leading sponsor of radical research and wrote *Pentagon Capitalism: The Political Economy of War*, a book published in 1970 and praised highly in *The New York Review of Books* by his political colleague, Robert L. Heilbroner, a Socialist Scholar.

Portage County Prosecutor Ronald J. Kanes, on 5/15/70, holds up an antique dagger, one of sixty assorted knives confiscated from dormitory rooms at Kent State University. A search of rooms vacated after four KSU students were shot to death 5/4/70 turned up a small number of guns, knives and drugs. UPI

SOCIALIST AUTHOR OF "OVERKILL"

Prof. Melman invented the propaganda concept that our nation has an excess "overkill" number of defense weapons for retaliation against a first strike Soviet attack. On January 5, 1964, the *New York Times* reported about a Congressional debate on the subject:

". . . Pentagon sources have not wholly accepted the 'overkill' argument put forward by some members of Congress, led by Senator George McGovern, Democrat of South Dakota. . . .

"Many supporters of the 'overkill' theory have based their views on a privately prepared report, under the leadership of Prof. Seymour Melman of Columbia University."

When Seymour Melman wrote his book *The Peace Race* in 1961, he proposed that our major factories for armaments, such as those operated by the Atomic Energy Commission "should be closed down completely." Prof. Melman went on, "I propose the closing down of military research and development establishments." Throughout our country, radical students belonging to Students for a Democratic Society and other revolutionary groups have been spurred into attacks on our campus military research and development centers by the writings of professors such as Seymour Melman, Socialist "scholar" and sponsor of SDS Radical Education Project. His influence is very strong, for he is professor of industrial engineering and management at Columbia University and enjoys wide access to information about our military-industrial complex, which constitutes the foundation of our national defense.

WRONG PREDICTION BY RED

Another original sponsor of SDS Radical Education Project is Victor Perlo, long-time Communist who was identified by the Senate Internal Security Subcommittee as a member of an espionage cell in the United States Government in World War II that operated in behalf of the Soviet Union. In 1960, Perlo spent three months there and interviewed Anastas I. Mikoyan in the Kremlin on August first. Thereafter, Perlo returned home to write *How The Soviet Economy Works—An Interview with A.I. Mikoyan* for International Publishers, the official Communist publishers. They described it as currently "the most authoritative interview concerning Soviet planning and economic questions obtained by an American . . . It explains fundamental features of economic policy and methods which represent the new roads the Soviet economy is treading."

An excellent example of Socialist Scholar Victor Perlo's radical scholarship is on page 20 of his book in the following quotation of a question by Perlo and an answer by Mikoyan:

Q. "What is the significance of the 20-Year Plan that is now being worked on?"

A. "The 20-Year Plan will be the skeleton of a new Party program. It will be ready in 1961. Certain figures are already in existence, but they are the raw materials for the plan. The scope is already set out in one of Premier Khrushchev's reports—that we expect to double American production by 1980."

Socialist economist Victor Perlo bought the Soviet 20-Year Plan lock, stock and barrel. Three years later, Khrushchev suddenly was deposed as Premier of the Soviet Union. Today its most fanatical and optimistic leaders do not even mention the prospect of catching up with, much less surpassing, American production in this century.

And so it goes.

JOURNEY TO HANOI

Howard Zinn, original sponsor of the SDS Radical Education Project, is a professor of political science at Boston University and author of *The Politics of History* (1970) which *New York Times* critic Christopher Lehmann-Haupt reviewed, May 4, 1970. He wrote:

"Specifically, Mr. Zinn makes the case for a radical approach to history. . . . In saying so he assaults the traditional view that the historical scholar's function is to be 'disinterested, objective, neutral, scientific, disengaged' and concerned only with his own 'discipline.'

"Instead, according to Mr. Zinn, the historian must recognize that in the very act of selecting a portion of the past for study from a certain point of view, he is exercising a strong bias toward the present. Since this is so, it follows that the scholar should investigate the past with an eye to becoming an actor in the present. . . ."

Professor Zinn is typical of the radical Marxist teachers of destruction. They do investigate the past for the purpose of becoming actors in the present. They conduct their investigation, however, in order to indict the past mercilessly and to become revolutionary actors of the kind exemplified by Daniel Berrigan, present Federal penitentiary inmate, with whom Professor Howard Zinn traveled to Hanoi in 1970 to "receive" three American fliers released by North Vietnam. The two did so, not in accordance with the Geneva Convention on Prisoners of War, but in accordance with the Communists' propaganda policy of lending prestige to anyone useful as a tool for their aims because of willingness to oppose publicly the aims of his or her own non-Communist or anti-Communist governments, as Zinn and Berrigan have done.

ESPIONAGE AGAINST U.S. BUSINESS

All the "research" of the SDS Radical Education Project is directed against the past and present of the United States Government, and against our free, private and competitive American economic system. So is all the "research" conducted by the SDS-REP affiliate organization, the North American Congress on Latin America (NACLA).

Its "Research Methodology Guide" by Lois Reivich, Michael Locker and Edie Black was widely distributed at the Fourth Annual Conference of Socialist Scholars, Rutgers, September 1968. The announced target of the guide is "The Empire," meaning every U.S. company and corporation doing business abroad, especially in Latin America, and all U.S. Government agencies dealing with our domestic and foreign economic and military operations. The NACLA guide is a recipe for espionage and sabotage.

Part One is entitled "Researching The Empire—How to Research the Imperial Elite: Corporations/People/Non-Profit Organizations/Government Agencies/Universities." Part Two is entitled "Campus Reconnaissance—How to Investigate Campus Military Contracting." Here are excerpts from both parts of the NACLA guide:

Page 1: "Interviews should be conducted after doing initial research; i.e., when you know what questions to ask and to whom to ask them.

"The interviewer should play a straight role, e.g., as a student doing research for a course paper.

"If the interview is conducted in such a manner that the interviewee is not threatened, he or she will usually be more than happy to talk.

Pages 11, 12: "Throughout Asia, Africa and Latin America a power struggle of monumental proportions is being waged between revolutionaries and U.S. technology. . . .

"The military-industrial complex is relying heavily on the innovative abilities of the academic world for defeating revolutionary solutions . . .

"Given such a situation, radicals and revolutionaries who want to crystalize the real issues involved in government-sponsored projects must zero in on the direct role such 'academic work' plays in wars against national liberation. . . .

Page 17: "Field Work

"At times interviews and observation can not be directly undertaken without creating a role that legitimizes their necessity. Covers can be easily erected by getting a friendly faculty member to authorize the research through a course or enlisting the aid of a campus newspaper reporter. In some situations where security is tight inside informers will be the only way to secure vital information. Personal contact with friends or political associates who have positions providing access to the information (i.e., secretaries, research assistants) can prove quite helpful. If necessary someone may have to take a job on the project or in the research facility to gain access to such information. Persons in positions of public authority, such as federal or state congressmen, senators, executive officials and their assistants, can easily acquire restricted (but not necessarily classified) information and forward it to you. Their desire to do so is usually proportional to the effect it might have on their own political well-being. Whatever the method, the problem of getting inside information (no matter its classifications) essentially involves finding a person with legitimacy in the authority's eyes who has access to the material and can transmit the data either secretly or without the threat of reprisal. Obviously such a person should be handled with discretion and the smaller the number of persons who know about it the better your chances of success."

It is true that our marvelous military-industrial complex relies heavily on the great creativity and innovative abilities of our brilliant engineers, scientists, technologists and mathematicians for invention of the methods and means enabling us to defend ourselves against Marxist "revolutionary solutions" to world problems.

That is why Socialist professors created a pro-Soviet "peace" movement in our country long before the Korean and Vietnam Wars, and have sought ever since 1945 to nullify our American military superiority through unilateral U.S. disarmament. For example, several present-day Socialist Scholars, all current sponsors or advisers to various members of the SDS Radical Education Project and its affiliate, the North American Congress on Latin America, were sponsors of the 1949 Waldorf Peace Conference in New York City—among them Herbert Aptheker, Corliss Lamont, Dr. Linus Pauling and Paul M. Sweezy. That conference was then publicly described as "pro-Communist" by Secretary of State Dean Acheson.

PROFESSORS AID INFILTRATION

Today, "radical researchers" belonging to REP and NACLA are indeed following their "methodology guide" to the letter. Backed by "friendly" faculty members at various universities, REP and NACLA researchers are obtaining "covers" enabling them to infiltrate government-sponsored projects, Congressional offices, industrial corporations and civic enterprises.

For so long as we Americans maintain the concept that our Constitutional First Amendment is a grant of absolute license for "anything goes" politically on the part of university faculty members, we shall have no legal protection from on-campus and off-campus violence triggered by teachers of destruction training students in the kind of "research" required for detonating social and physical explosions, in the manner that fugitive-from-justice Pat Swinton of NACLA is charged with having done when she took part in bombing buildings in New York City, a criminal act for which her four companions already have been tried and pleaded "guilty."

Chapter 15

REVOLUTIONARIES' INTENTIONS

ON APRIL 28, 1970, the Steering Committee of the Socialist Scholars sent out a letter notifying the membership that the customary date of the group's annual conference would be advanced by three months, and that instead of being held in September at a university, the Sixth Annual Conference of Socialist Scholars would be held over the weekend of June 13-14, 1970, at Intermediate School Number 70 on West 17th Street in Manhattan.

The reason for advancing the date of the conference was purely political, as can be seen in the following text from the Steering Committee's letter:

"This year's conference reflects a number of changes in the SSC (including a change in date—June rather than September). Although continuing to present panels intended to analyze methodological and substantive questions, the program also includes panels directly concerned with issues of immediate political relevance. Participating, as in the past, will be a number of well-known Marxists, but there will also be many younger intellectuals and political activists.

"This broadened conception of the conference is the result of our revised analysis of the possibilities of building a socialist movement in America, and our assessment of the role that the SSC can play in that development.

"The general if only implied assumption of those who founded the SSC five years ago was that American Capitalism had entered a period of long-run stability, eliminating the possibility of any mass socialist opposition. . . .

"The last five years, however, has [sic] witnessed a rapid disintegration of Bourgeois [middle class] hegemony in many aspects of American life. While the state remains strong and relatively unshaken, other aspects of civil society have lost much of their force, providing the opportunity for socialist attack."

The Socialist Scholars' diagnosis of the present condition of our society is, in my opinion, entirely correct. Since their first conference in 1965, there has indeed occurred such rapid disintegration of middle-class authority in the United States that today almost every ethically firm foundation of our cultural, spiritual and moral life is severely shaken and perhaps permanently undermined. Elated, the Socialist Scholars and their Marxist radical associates now believe they can soon move in for the final wrecking operation.

The Socialist Scholars Conference letter of April 28 went on to say that many socialist scholars once isolated on college campuses have become involved in political movements and there has emerged a significant group of "activist intellectuals" who are relating their intellectual functions to building a socialist movement. "These developments," declared the SSC Steering Committee, "make it possible for the SSC to play a more direct role: to support and influence the growth of an American Socialist Movement."

The official June 1970 SSC program carried most revealing notes about the various panel sessions. For example, it stated about the panel on the ruling classes:

"Charles Wheatley (Princeton University)—An examination of the forms and degrees of operational unity among elite elements supports the assertion that there is essential unity among all major institutional elites."

Four months earlier, Assistant Professor Charles W. Wheatley of the Princeton University sociology department had acted as treasurer of a "Repression Teach-In" at Dillon Gymnasium where 3,000 professors, students and outsiders were harangued by Leonard Weinglass, one of the Chicago Conspiracy Seven lawyers charged with contempt of court;

by Felipe Luciano, member of the Young Lords, a Puerto Rican counterpart of the Black Panthers; and by David Hilliard, a leader of the Black Panthers.

RHETORIC ON PRINCETON CAMPUS

The deterioration of middle-class morality and authority has been so rapid and acute at Princeton under President Robert Goheen that David Hilliard was permitted to proclaim on campus: "So for all the pigs in the audience—for all the pigs wherever they are and they're everywhere—we have to relate to that—we want to tell them that yes we're subversive, and yes we do intend to overthrow the United States Government. . . . You have to recognize, you have to realize, that the true symbols of fascism is [sic] not manifested in Adolf Hitler, that the true symbols of fascism is manifested in the American Eagle and the American Flag."

For that, David Hilliard was paid an honorarium of $2,000 raised by the Princeton Faculty-Staff Teach-In Support Group. Its co-chairmen were Stanley J. Stein, Stuart Hampshire, Ernest Gordon and Marvin Bressler. At the teach-in, Charles W. Wheatley solicited contributions for the speakers who—he said—"can do the job we know has to be done."

At the Sixth Annual Conference of Socialist Scholars, June 14, 1970, the moderator for the panel on "The Old Right and The New Left" was Ronald Radosh of Queensborough Community College. He introduced Dr. Murray N. Rothbard of Brooklyn Polytechnic Institute by commenting on an editorial in the *New York Times* of that day, a reprint of Robert L. Duffus' "What's A Flag?". Mr. Radosh made snide remarks about our flag and went on to say that Murray Rothbard once described the flag as "a rag." The latter made no objection to Ronald Radosh's introduction.

It is not surprising that Dr. Rothbard and Leonard P. Liggio appeared together on the same Socialist Scholars Conference panel. A semi-monthly newsletter, *The Libertarian Forum*, of which Murray N. Rothbard is editor, carries in its May 15, 1970 issue the article "The State of the

A policeman disarms a youth carrying a pistol at Kent State University campus on 5/4/70. Four persons were reported killed and others wounded when National Guardsmen fired into crowd on the commons after anti-war demonstrators hurled rocks at them.   UPI

Movement" by Leonard P. Liggio with the following editorial note:

"We are proud to reserve this issue for an article on the state of the Left by Professor Leonard P. Liggio. Of all the libertarians [sic!] in this country, Leonard Liggio has had the closest long-time association with the New Left and with its most important publications. In the light of this special knowledge, Professor Liggio's analysis of the current state of the Left takes on particular importance. Leonard Liggio teaches history at the City University of New York."

An example of Prof. Liggio's "libertarian" thinking can be found in the following quote from his article of May 15, 1970: "With native American genius the SDS [revolutionary communist Students for a Democratic Society] opted for direct opposition to U.S. imperialism—by confrontation with the draft. Coming from within the American people, they did not fear the Justice Department, Federal Courts or the rest of the U.S. apparatus of repression."

In a sense, editor Rothbard is correct in his estimate of Leonard Liggio's article as extremely important. It contains a judgment about the state of "The Movement" that seems to have been the main theme of the Socialist Scholars Sixth Annual Conference.

Prof. Liggio quotes and endorses highly the "excellent analysis" by the "ever-thoughtful" Julius Lester who, in rebuking the Black Panthers for having formed a separate political action party, wrote:

"It takes more than guts to make a revolution, it takes more than courage to risk one's life for an ideal. It takes more than a willingness to die, it takes sense enough to know when to say 'advance' and when to say 'retreat.' It takes sense enough to know what your organization can do and what it can't do. Because one has a gun and some bullets doesn't mean to go out and shoot a cop. Cops, guns and bullets are not in short supply. They'll be there whenever one is ready. . . Prior to that, however, one needs to build himself a base, so that when he proceeds to shoot that cop, he has minimized as much as possible the dangers of losing his own life. . . ."

To know when to advance and when to retreat, to find out how to build a base for mass violent revolutionary action, to analyze correctly the given conditions in a given situation within a specific country—all these who-what-when-where-and-how problems have been the principal concern of Marxists since first publication of "The Communist Manifesto."

Their basic aim is always the same: to set up a worldwide proletarian dictatorship "by the forcible overthrow of all existing social conditions." To accomplish that aim, all Marxists in non-Communist nations regard their work as only "the prelude" to seizure of state power. During the prelude, they form various kinds of associations to achieve their objective—united fronts, popular fronts, activist cadres, anarchic terrorist corps. "In short," as Marx and Engels put it plainly in the Manifesto, "the Communists everywhere support every revolutionary movement against the existing social and political order of things. In all these movements they bring to the front, as the leading question in each case, the property question, no matter what its degree of development at the time."

That is precisely what the Socialist Scholars have been doing since 1965 and are now doing in our country. They are working with *every* revolutionary movement in the United States and abroad against the existing American social and political order of things. And always, the efforts are directed at the *property* question, trying to wrest control of property away from any and all private hands.

SIGNIFICANT POSITION PAPER

All the foregoing strategy, tactics and aims were set forth at length and with complete clarity in the position paper "Towards a Socialist Strategy for the United States" that was distributed to those in attendance at the Socialist Scholars Conference in June 1970, and is now being circulated throughout the New Politics movement.

As usual, there has been no critical discussion and analysis of the document by the big press or Congress, though the position paper is as pertinent to our American situation in the 1970's as *Mein Kampf* was to the German situation in the 1930's. In some ghastly way, it seems to be foreordained in our age of instant communications that the most important news is least known.

Evidently it is not persuasive now to recall Winston Churchill's trenchant statement that if two men had read one book, the history of the world might have been different, meaning that if Daladier of France and Chamberlain of Great Britain had read *Mein Kampf*, they would not have signed the Munich Pact with Hitler in September 1938, a "peace" agreement which anyone familiar with his written plans would have known was bound to be interpreted by him as a green light for military aggression.

Similarly, if one man had read one book before February 1945, meaning if President Franklin D. Roosevelt had read Joseph Stalin's *Marxism and the National and Colonial Question,* the United States would not have reached agreements with Stalin at Yalta that lost the peace after World War II was won, that put East Europe behind an Iron Curtain, that brought on the Cold War and no-win Korean and Vietnam Wars, and could be the origin of World War III.

Only the initiated read the uncensored version of *Mein Kampf* and acted on it. They conquered almost all of Europe and were defeated at a cost of lives, blood, sweat and tears too great to count. Only the initiated read the uncensored version of *Marxism and the National and Colonial Question* and acted on it. They conquered and enslaved a third of the world. Only the initiated are reading "Towards a Socialist Strategy for the United States" and are acting on it. Possibly, they will conquer our country, the citadel of a besieged Western civilization.

It is imperative now, in my judgment, for our best minds to study the American Marxists' current position paper, so that means can be devised to thwart their strategy. But, as the great French historian Pierre Gaxotte of the *Academie Francaise* explains, leaders in the West are so busy going places, doing things, keeping appointments and taking part in endless dialogue, that they have no time, apparently, to sit

John Plimpton, a salesman at The Brass Rail in Los Angeles, a local gunshop, holds up a .380 Browning automatic pistol similar to the one he says he sold to ousted U C L A professor Angela Davis on January 12, 1970. He holds up a photo of Miss Davis August 10th and next to it has the Firearm Purchase or Registration Report of the sale, signed by Miss Davis. The San Francisco Examiner said that two of the guns used in a San R a f a e l , Calif. shootout which took the lives of a judge and three other persons the week before, were purchased originally by Miss Davis.

down and study what most needs to be studied—the current strategy of our Marxist enemies. Yet without accurate knowledge of that strategy, it is impossible to defeat it.

At some future point in time, I predict, if our present form of government has been overthrown and replaced by a dictatorship of some kind, those Americans who remember what it was like to live in freedom, who are hankering after it, and are wondering how they lost it, will read "Towards a Socialist Strategy for the United States" by Frank Brodhead, Edward Greer, Amy Kesselman, Karl Klare and Ruth Meyerowitz.

They explain in their first paragraph, "This document was written by a group of independent movement people doing community organizing --- --- ---- in New Haven, Chicago and Cambridge, Mass. Its purpose is to bring together the strands of the new left analysis of American society and to attempt to articulate the politics of that tendency within socialist thought."

Between "organizing" and "in New Haven" in the first sentence of the position paper, three words were inked out by hand before distribution to the Socialist Scholars Conference. Significantly, the inked-out words—easily decipherable—are "and SDS work."

Obviously, the criminal activities of the Weatherman faction of Students for a Democratic Society (SDS)—the setting up of bomb factories and destruction of buildings by arson—have made almost all Socialist Scholars and their fellow travelers wary of open association with SDS. Moreover, the strong reaction of the Building and Construction Trades Union workers, the "hard hats," first in New York City and then in other big cities, has jolted the Left and forced many Marxists to face the reality of how alienated they really are from the mass of working people in the United States.

On the other hand, the Marxists are extremely influential with some members of our Supreme Court and among the intellectuals dominating most of our universities, communications media and tax-exempt foundations. In addition, the Marxists are highly influential, perhaps fashionable is more correct, among many of our very well-to-do or wealthy citizens dabbling in intellectualism and revolution.

SOCIALIST PLANS—WITH COMMENTARY

The 23-page 1970 position paper "Towards a Socialist Strategy for the United States" is divided into sections. The following principal points quoted *verbatim* from it are accompanied by my own parenthetic comments:

"SOCIALISM

". . . The creation of a truly socialist society requires a redefinition of man as well as a new model of civilization . . .

"As described by Lenin in 'State and Revolution,' socialism requires abolishing the distinction between the rulers and the governed. It demands daily participation and decision-making by all members of the society at every level—the state, at the work place, and in the social life of the community. . . ."

(What the New Left means today by "participatory democracy" is Leninist-type "democracy," not Jeffersonian democracy. Even an indoctrinated Communist such as Alexander Dubcek of Czechoslovakia resembled other Marxian politicians under the illusion that the Communist International tolerates genuine participatioñ in decision-making by individuals not belonging to the ruling elite in Moscow and Peiping. Dubcek found out the truth concerning Leninist participatory democracy in the fall of 1968, when the Soviet Union sent tanks into Czechoslovakia to put down his attempted participation in governing the People's Democratic Republic of Czechoslovakia.)

"But the material wealth and highly advanced technology of the United States offers a unique opportunity for achieving a humane socialism. In particular, the absence of the material constraints for building a socialist society means that the model of 'forced industrialization' and 'primitive accumulation' associated with the Stalinist era will not be the model for revolution in America. . . .Indeed, the dominant position and great wealth of American capitalism dictates [sic] that American socialism will have a particular world role—the dismantling of the present system of world imperialism."

(The dominant position and great wealth of our country have been attained under capitalism. If it were to be destroyed, America, under socialism, would stagnate and then retrogress. According to Marx and Lenin, imperialism is the most advanced stage of capitalism; the New Left envisions a Socialist United States as the world leader in dismantling advanced capitalism. Many Americans who are sincerely anti-colonialist make the mistake of believing that Marxists regard "colonialism" and "imperialism" as synonymous. They do not. All private foreign capital investment is regarded by Marxists as "imperialist;" all aid extended to a foreign nation by a non-socialist nation is regarded as "imperialist." The U.S. massive aid to Peruvians after the 1970 earthquake was described by Marxists as "imperialist," but Soviet token aid to Peruvians was described as "humanitarian" and "fraternal." Marxists describe Soviet military and economic aid to Egypt as part of the "democratic liberation movement;" they describe American military and economic aid to the Philippine Republic as "imperialist oppression.")

"HISTORY

"Although we can begin to develop the outline of socialist relationships now, we can only complete the construction of a socialist society after power has been taken from those who live off, profit from, and have an interest in maintaining the Capitalist system.

". . . Thus, the struggle against imperialism is an integral part of the struggle for socialism in America. Our movement must be seen (both theoretically and programmatically) as inextricably linked to the world revolution: the two are in fact part of the same struggle. . . .

"STRATEGY

". . . In actual practice, each 'tier' of society—social relations, ideological and cultural life, domestic and

international politics—has a relatively autonomous existence of its own. . . .

"Thus, we believe that the working class is the central
focus of a revolutionary strategy for the United States and
any socialist revolution must be broadly and actively
based in the working class. Having said this, we must guard
against the tendency of the Movement to view the
working class monolithically and as somehow distinct from
the sectors which comprise it—women, blacks, youth,
industrial workers, service workers, white-collar strata:
that is, all groups of people who sell their labor power.

"THE REVOLUTIONARY PROCESS

"We wish to distinguish between two phases of the
revolutionary process: the social or cultural revolution,
and the seizure of state power. . . .

"1. *Permanent Social Revolution.* By this we mean a
broad social and cultural transformation, based on a total
critique of life under capitalism. . . .

"2. *Seizure of State Power.* As a last resort, and often
sooner, the capitalist class will use its control of the state
apparatus to suppress revolutionary activity. Thus, to
carry through the revolution, it will be necessary to seize
and dismantle the bourgeois state apparatus and to replace
it by political forms which represent the working class."

(Joseph Stalin, whose personality but not political writings
have been downgraded by the Kremlin elite, explained in a
speech to the Central Control Commission of the Communist
Party of the Soviet Union, August 1, 1927, "Whoever does
not understand that there are no revolutions without definite
stages of development. . .understands nothing of Marxism."

(We in the United States today are in the first phase of the
Marxist revolution, the phase of the social and cultural
revolution based on Marxists' "total critique" of the quality
of life under capitalism and of all our institutions. Trying to
appease Marxists or to dissuade them, many open-minded
Americans—not recognizing the totality of socialist
opposition to everything we think, say, do, create and make
in our society—readily concede the existence of faults and
injustices in our way of life and offer to cooperate with

anyone seeking to correct them. Cooperating with Marxists to try to cure the ills of our society is like cooperating with a Typhoid Mary to cure a hospital patient.

(Of course our society has grave faults sorely needing correction and serious ills requiring remedies. But Marxists do not really want to improve or reform it within its extant framework. They merely try to manipulate our natural moral and emotional disapproval of the weaknesses and ills in our society as a tool for obtaining total rejection of it. Figuratively speaking, they suggest giving a baby a much needed bath so that the baby can be thrown out with the bath water. They don't want any part of the baby as he is. The only baby they want is one conceived, born, brought up and ruled by Marxism. That is the brutal fact confronting the appeasers and effete intellectuals in our country, a fact so brutal they refuse to believe it.)

"STRATEGY IN THE AMERICAN CONTEXT

". . . it is clear that the primary strategic perspective of American socialism should be to launch the social and cultural revolution on all fronts. This means desanctifying and putting into crisis all capitalist institutions and social relationships.

"This does not mean we ignore the question of state power. . . . Nevertheless, we believe that actually *contesting for state power* is only on the long-run agenda of the American revolution.

"In the discussion of strategy. . .we are focusing primarily on the white New Left movements. . . .In the case of black people the situation is clear—the government is bent on destroying leadership elements like the Black Panther Party. . .In the face of this the Movement's need to confront the courts and the state, not only defensively but offensively as well, is obvious. . . "

(Though startling and shocking to most Americans, there is nothing new about present day Marxists' defiance of our courts and attempts to embarrass, discredit and destroy our traditional Anglo-Saxon judicial system. In the early days of the Soviet Union, at the Third Congress of the Communist International in Moscow, 1921, Elena Stasova, international secretary, announced, "We decided it was necessary to publish a pamphlet 'How To Act When Arrested and Questioned' ". Subsequently, the International Labor Defense in New York City issued an American adaptation of that Communist pamphlet entitled "Under Arrest!" It states:

"The dignity and sanctity of the courts are a means of paralyzing the struggle of the workers [Marxist revolutionaries] against the capitalist institutions. . . . The worker must understand that the courts are not impartial, any more than any other agency of capitalist government is impartial. . . . The worker must realize that the charge against him is only a legal frame-up. . . . Even though capitalist law makes what you have done a crime, you must plead 'not guilty.' . . . By the strength of your cause, make capitalism the defendant and yourself the prosecutor. . . . It is important that you insist on answering questions put to you in your own way. . . You either answer your own way or not at all. . . . Capitalism is guilty of force and violence. . . . Demand a working class jury; get up and challenge the entire panel of prospective jurors on the ground that it is composed of people whose social and economic interests will prejudice them against you, the defendant. . . . You should also state that workers expect no justice in a capitalist court. A most important consideration of workers' self-defense is to use the capitalist courtroom as a forum. . . . On the date of the trial there should take place a demonstration in front of the courthouse. A leaflet should be issued in which should be set forth simply and briefly the arrest of the worker and the issue involved. The leaflet should. . . announce a mass meeting to protest against the worker's arrest. In the course of this mass meeting. . . a short but vigorous resolution should be adopted and sent to the local officials and the press, and should demand the immediate and unconditional release of the arrested worker."

(As readers can see, every instruction in "Under Arrest!" has been followed to the letter by the defendants in the 1969 Chicago Conspiracy Seven trial and in the 1970 New Haven Black Panther trial. The original instructions for defense of arrested Marxist revolutionaries that were published by the Third Congress of the Communist International have been scrupulously followed in every case involving an arrested Communist or revolutionary Marxist — no matter how horrible the nature of his or her crime — everywhere in the world since 1921.

(Soon after Charles de Gaulle became President of France in 1958, forty Parisian intellectuals, led by Marxist radicals Jean Paul Sartre and Simone Beauvoir, took part in such a violent street demonstration on behalf of a convicted and sentenced Communist murderer, and conducted such an intensive propaganda campaign on his behalf over radio and television, that De Gaulle banned the "40 intellectuals" from the government-owned airwaves, saying he would not permit them to use a government forum on behalf of a common criminal.

(When President Kingman Brewster Jr. of Yale University stated publicly in reference to the 1970 Black Panther trial in New Haven that he is "skeptical" about a black man's being able to receive a fair trial in the United States, he was mouthing the kind of propaganda put forth in the Communist pamphlet "Under Arrest!" almost fifty years ago. That same kind of propaganda was afforded a forum in actress Jane Fonda's penthouse apartment in Manhattan where, at a press conference on August 22, 1970, Black Panther "defense minister" Huey Newton warned of "military action against the entire court system" in our country unless Panther Lonnie McLucas, standing trial for murder, were "vindicated" by the New Haven court. He also ordered a Black Panther sit-in in the courtroom during the New Haven trial to intimidate the jurors.

(Brilliantly, the Marxist revolutionaries in our country, all well schooled by Socialist professors and their academic associates, have succeeded in capturing almost the entire communications media as a front page or prime time radio and television forum. Tragically for our nation, that forum for violent Marxist propaganda was set up when the Warren Supreme Court struck down, in the name of freedom of speech, almost all the provisions of our internal security laws.

(It is a weird historical development that a nation founded in the 18th century Age of Enlightenment by thinkers skeptical of the divine right of kings is being forced into anarchy in the 20th century Age of Derangement by believers in the divine rightness of Karl Marx and in the intellectual, ideological and judicial infallibility of Supreme Court Justices Earl Warren, Hugo Black and William O. Douglas.)

"IMPLEMENTATION
THE INTERMEDIATE STRATEGY

". . .A first step in the intermediate strategy is to help launch anti-capitalist reform struggle on all fronts. . .We must articulate demands from a new set of priorities and values, based on a total vision antagonistic to the logic of capitalism. . .

"Above all, our demands must go beyond the boundaries of what is 'realistic' in the system,. . .For example, a collective of working women would not just demand equal wages with men. . .They would also demand a day-care center provided by the employer, under the control of the women, with time off for supervision and participation. . . .

"Similarly, in the area of public education, we must challenge the entire quality of that education. At the high school level, we should attack the tracking system as an embodiment of the class structure of society. . . .We should not limit our demands to higher teacher/pupil ratios, but challenge the whole authoritarian and dehumanizing structure of the classroom relationship. . . . At the college level the demand for open admission challenges the class and racist nature of the university.

"An important possibility for the future will be the growth of a workers' control movement. At issue would be not only wages, but the entire character of the work relationship, especially the right of the boss to determine the level of production and the allocation of the surplus regardless of the impact on the workers and their families. (A draft discussion paper by the Boston Labor Study Group contains numerous examples of challenges to the company's 'right to manage.')"

(What so many goodhearted, idealistic and well-meaning people fail to perceive today in our country, wherein all sorts of demands are being made by members of the New Politics movement for instant reform of our entire society, is that they initiate these demands merely as a first anti-capitalist step, just as Ralph Nader's reform consumerism in his bestseller *Unsafe At Any Speed* against a car manufactured by General Motors was a first step in his radical program to challenge GM's "right to manage.")

"DUAL POWER

". . . the intermediate strategy calls for the development of an autonomous network of institutions of popular power. Dual power institutions should be deeply imbedded in the institutions of capitalist society. They should exist in the workplace (e.g., workers' councils), in the public schools (e.g., student-teacher-parent groups based on community control of the schools), and in the universities (e.g. school strike committees). . . . .

"The purpose of dual power is twofold. First, it contests the power of the ruling class . . . Second, the institutions of dual power must be the prototype of the radically democratic political forms of the future. . . .

"The strategy of dual power should not be confused with the development of 'counter-institutions' — coffee-houses, free universities, underground newspapers. These latter play an important role in ideological and cultural confrontation."

(The New Left coffeehouses near U.S. armed forces installations, the "free" off-campus radical universities and the underground newspapers have been largely responsible for incidents of violence on and off campus during recent years.)

"However, these [counter] institutions . . .are not in-volved in contesting power as such. To rely solely on counter-institutions as a *strategy* would be dangerously utopian.

"We are not proposing the notion that we can accumulate little islands within capitalism secure from bourgeois power, that one day these will have expanded enough to include 51% of the power in society, and that this will then constitute victory. This conception leads to the reformist fallacy that the capitalist class will give up without a struggle . . . We must be prepared for ups and downs, ebbs and flows, and the rapid escalation and de-escalation of intense crises. . . ."

"THE ARTICULATION OF RESISTANCE CULTURE

"The new social relationships and participatory institutions . . . will amount to the creation of a new resistance culture. The extensions and generalization of this culture must be a priority for our movement . . . We must wage struggles on the ideological, artistic, and intellectual levels. . . "

(The cultural barbarism of a Marxist type such as a Nikita Khrushchev can easily be understood. When he harangued the world's leading journalists at the Palais de Chaillot in Paris for two and a half hours, at the time of the aborted summit conference of May 1960 — pouring forth a stream of four-letter-word obscenities so vile that he even told a dirty story about his own mother — it was obvious that he is, as a member of the French Ministry of Information told me, "a vulgar thug." As such, he threatened to "rain rockets on the Parthenon." Why not? It has absolutely no meaning for him. When a French Government guide, a charming young woman, showed the Cathedral of Chartres to Khrushchev, during his 1960 winter visit to France, he was not only bored but also rude. Standing on the steps leading to the marvelous cathedral facade, he turned his back to it, gestured at the French countryside, and said to the guide, "Show me an onion, or a cabbage."

(The cultural barbarism of a Marxist such as a Socialist Scholar or member of "The Movement" in our country today springs, however, from a different origin than Khrushchev's, for it is intentional and the purveyors of that barbarism — from "Woodstock Nation" to "Myra Breckinridge," from "Soul on Ice" to "Do It!" — are willful and venal annihilators.

(Khrushchev speaks coarse Russian because he can't speak it well or correctly; David Dellinger, a Yale University graduate, speaks coarse four-letter-word English to degrade our language and society.)

"PROSPECTS

"... Even though the United States is not in a revolutionary situation, there are growing prospects for a socialist movement... These prospects stem from two inter-connected sources: the contradictions of American imperialism in the world arena and the crisis of domestic society...

"In the international arena the Vietnamese revolution is the critical world event of this era. The heroic resistance of the Vietnamese people has demonstrated that American imperialism can be defeated. This will lead, as Ché [Guevara] urged, to the spread of wars of national liberation."

(Let all misguided "peace" advocates take note of this loud and clear warning from the enemy within our midst, an enemy openly connected with the world socialist revolution. An immediate withdrawal of all U.S. forces from Vietnam, or an abandonment of South Vietnam, will mean only one thing—more Communist-instigated wars!)

"..the Nixon Administration will have to begin to systematically repress the Movement.

"..This will not be a crude form of repression; it is unlikely the government will suddenly send every protestor to concentration camps. It will be highly sophisticated and expert: destruction of the black leadership, quiet but persistent imprisonment of white revolutionaries, the use of all kinds of 'non-political' judicial techniques (such as convictions on drug charges, conspiracy, etc.), propaganda campaigns, intimidation of the media, and so on.

"In the face of this it is clear that the Movement is in a dilemma. We do not now have a mass base ... On the other hand, our confrontations with state power are becoming every-day occurrences. Accordingly an immediate and pressing priority, to which many in the Movement have begun to devote themselves, is the development of strategies for dealing with repression. These must have both a defensive aspect (to keep our brothers out of jail) and a 'cultural revolution' aspect—that is, they must desanctify the courts, expose them as agencies of class-justice, and give people the courage to carry on the struggle.

"An organized revolutionary leadership will be required to bring coherence to the movement.. . . .It follows that the American revolution requires a new type of organization and political leadership.

"The functions of revolutionary leadership are theoretical analysis, socialist education, political leadership, and exemplary action. . . .

"In a society as differentiated as ours, various sectors will advance politically at different rates. . . .A revolutionary party must fuse together all oppressed sectors of society into what Antonio Gramsci called 'a revolutionary bloc.'

"A bloc is not an alliance. . . .an alliance is a temporary accord between sectors or classes. . . .A bloc demands representing the lowest common political denominator. A bloc is a synthesis of the demands of all sectors into a unified and universal critique of capitalism. . . .

"Recently, movement activists interested in working toward a revolutionary party have turned to the only hitherto successful model, the Leninist 'cadre' party . . . This is unfortunate, since, as we shall argue, the Bolshevik model is entirely inappropriate to our needs. (It is important to underscore this since new left activists of our generation tend not to know the Bolshevik model in its original form, but are more familiar with its Stalinist deformation.). . .

"An important characteristic of recent movements for social change is the revolt against bureaucracy. . . .

"To implement the strategies necessary to lead to the liberation of specially oppressed sectors of American society (e.g., blacks, women), these groups must have political and cultural autonomy within any organizational forms to be established. . . .

"No single sector of the movement can determine the shape of the new party. A party launched by the new left at the present time would necessarily slight the interests of blacks, third world groups, women and workers.

"A revolutionary party, however, does not emerge spontaneously. . . .To wait for it to arrive is to deny the necessity of conscious initiatives in making history. . . .

"While stressing the diversity within the leadership, we should note that it cannot be *so* decentralized that it is unable to perform its coordinating and synthesizing role. We must not forget that the party is ultimately on the trajectory toward contesting state power....The 'organizer' rather than the 'cadre' is the model suited to this kind of party. Thus the type of vanguard party we have in mind is somewhere in between the traditional mass party and the elite cadre.

"The Bolshevik model was designed for the task of *seizing* state power from the authoritarian czarist dictatorship and presiding over the construction of socialism in an underdeveloped country. But the immediate task of the movement [in the United States] is the *social revolution* rather than the seizure of state power.

"Neither the special features of American capitalist power—racism, the totality of bourgeois hegemony, etc.—nor the strategic tasks of the social revolution set out above, point to the need for a Leninist party. Rather, the American revolution requires the definition and elaboration of a new type of vanguard party. To work out the form of that party is a task of our generation."

The foregoing last sentence, setting forth the New Politics movement's concept of its current task, is the end of the position paper "Towards a Socialist Strategy for the United States" that was distributed at the Sixth Annual Conference of Socialist Scholars in June 1970. As listed on the official SSC program, the participants were:

Margaret Benston, Simon Fraser University
Francine Blau Weisskoff, Harvard University
Jacqui Bernard, Member, Red Stockings
Charles W. Wheatley, Princeton University
Paul M. Sweezy, *Monthly Review*
Robert I. Rhodes, State University of New York at Binghamton
Edgar M. Branch, Miami University of Ohio
Richard Greeman, Wesleyan University
Jack A. Robbins, Fordham
Martin Corbin, *Catholic Worker*

Thomas Casey, Marist College

Joseph Cunneen, *Cross Currents*
Jerry McLoone, College of New Rochelle
Fred Ciporen, State University of New York at Old Westbury
Ronald Radosh, Queensborough Community College
Leonard Liggio, City College of New York
Raymond S. Franklin, Queens College
Paul Buhle, *Radical America*
Robert Langston, *The Militant*
Murray Bookchin, *Anarchos*
Mike Bass, Ecology Action East
Richard Friedman, Essex County College
Annette R. Rubinstein, *Science & Society*
Paul N. Siegel, Long Island University
Timothy Harding, California State College at Los Angeles
Marlene Dixon, McGill University
Roxanne Dunbar, "No More Fun and Games"
Evelyn Reed, "Problems of Women's Liberation"
Debbie Gerson
William Frain, College of New Rochelle
Louis Lipsitz, University of North Carolina
George Flannagan, Fordham University
Murray Rothbard, Polytechnic Institute of Brooklyn
Justus Doenecke, New College, Sarasota, Florida
Peter Roman, Princeton
Karl Klare, Adelphi College
Edward Greer, Wheaton College
Stanley Aronowitz

Speakers for Women's Liberation:

    Ann Ferrar
    Jenifer Gardner
    Lucille Iverson
    Sister Everyone
    Roberta Satow
Richard D. Wolff, City College of New York
Stephen Hymer, Yale University
Larry Sawers, American University
Jill Hamburg, U.P.A., Cambridge
Walter South, Richmond College
Elliott Sclar, Cambridge Institute

    Anticipation of the November 1970 elections in our
country was the basic reason why the Socialist Scholars

advanced the customary date of their annual conference by three months. Thus they could use the summer months for organization of political activism designed to influence the outcome of certain key contests in those elections, and lay the groundwork for fulfilling the revolutionary threat to our country.

As the position paper "Towards a Socialist Strategy for the United States" explains, Marxist teachers of destruction in our country do not expect to seize state power here in the near future. They do expect that in 1970 and 1971 they will be so successful in the first phase of their activities — the social and cultural revolution — that they can either force President Nixon to follow in President Johnson's footsteps and "abdicate" before November 1972, or force our nation into such a violent civil crisis, before and after the 1972 presidential elections, that the terrible events which took place during the 1968 Democratic National Convention in Chicago will seem relatively calm by contrast.

The Socialist Scholars' pupils view the future creation of an American revolutionary Marxist political party as the principal task of their generation.

It is the task of all freedom-loving Americans today, regardless of generation and of regular party affiliation, to protect our country from the two-phase socialist strategy: (1) the sabotage of our American way of life through social and cultural revolution; (2) the overthrow of our form of government by socialist seizure of state power.

DISBELIEF, OUR MAJOR OBSTACLE

From all my years of personal experience as an eyewitness to the internal subversion of our nation, I have concluded that our major obstacle in thwarting that subversion is the average American's natural inclination to believe the best about people and reluctance to believe that any American could wish to destroy our beloved country. It is an inclination and reluctance I myself share. Time and time again, after having attended radical meetings where I heard the Marxists plan our destruction with my own ears, and read their plans with my own eyes, I have come home tired, sick at heart, filled with revulsion over what I've seen and heard, and said to myself, "I just can't believe it!"

But all the evidence was there and I knew I'd better believe it, for the sake of all we hold dear — our civilization, our country, our children, grandchildren and succeeding generations.

Perhaps what I wish to express is best illustrated by the following true story:

At Vanderbilt University in Tennessee, Charles R. B. Stowe, a junior deeply concerned over false radical New Left propaganda circulated on campus, formed in 1969 an information service to present facts to students and solicited funds for it. Through a relative's acquaintance with the wife of an industrial company president, Charles was able to obtain an appointment with him, in March 1970, at his residence.

As Charles waited for the interview, he overheard the company president say to his wife, who had insisted he grant the appointment, "I spend my life at the office being pestered by people wanting this and that. Can't a man have a little peace and relaxation in his own home?"

Immediately after Charles had shaken hands, he said, "Sir, my father says if you have something to say, just put it in writing. So please, sir, here is something for you to read." Charles gave him a short summary of the aims and history of his student information service and some newspaper clippings about its work in trying to combat violent Marxist radicalism on and off campus.

The company president read the material in a polite, bored way. "So what?" he said.

Trying hard to make some kind of impression, Charles explained he is in Navy ROTC, is taking part in Volunteers for Service to help disadvantaged children improve their school work, and is writing and speaking out against New Left radical activity.

"Just how serious do you think it is?" said the company president, glancing at his watch and putting out a hand to say good-bye.

"Well, sir," burst out Charles, "New Left radicalism is so serious it could even cost you your life!"

The company president smiled, said he'd take another look at Charles' material sometime at the office, would see if he could make a small contribution to help the student information service, and ended the interview.

Next day, in the very early morning, the company president's offices high up in a Manhattan skyscraper were blown to bits in the New York City bombing that shook the nation and were perpetrated by young radicals of "Revolutionary Force 9."

EPILOGUE

Administrator's, Faculty Member's, and Law Officer's Responsibilities For Campus Order
by J. Edgar Hoover*

IN A VERY SHORT TIME our Nation's colleges and universities will begin their fall terms. Thousands of our finest young people will resume their pursuit of education that will enable them to better serve their communities and their country. These young men and women will soon be among those entrusted with the responsibility of leadership and the obligation of shaping the future direction of our Nation. It is imperative that their preparation for this most significant task be of the highest quality and that it be gained in an uninterrupted atmosphere conducive to educational excellence.

The responsibility for insuring that these goals are achieved rests squarely with college administrators. They alone, by setting guidelines of conduct, control the activities of their students. Let not the issue of student conduct be clouded by philosophical mouthings of self-determination, cries of repression, or claims of attack against intellectual freedom. College administrators must rise to face the issues honestly and then have the courage to firmly implement policies that will not permit or condone any illegitimate interruption of the educational process. This position must be maintained regardless of the dire consequences threatened by those who seek, either deliberately or through confused direction, to disrupt our institutions of higher learning.

The radicals who have plagued many of our colleges and universities know well that their success in part is dependent upon weak administrators—leaders who refuse to accept the responsibility of maintaining order. Certainly, unlimited freedom of students to disrupt or destroy and doubtful punish-

---

* Text appeared in the Sept 1, 1970 FBI Law Enforcement Bulletin

ment for such activity give great impetus to its continuation. College administrators across the land must unite in placing order on their individual campuses as the top priority item. Unruly students, of course, are not the only bane of college and university officials. Some faculty members act like rabid anarchists and spend most of their time encouraging enthusiastic but naive young people to overthrow established procedure. To some professors, academic freedom appears to mean freedom to destroy our educational processes. The disarrays of last spring must be replaced with firm, established policy designed to protect the entire student body and not just a vocal minority whose uncontrolled activities threaten the entire structure of higher education.

As law enforcement officers, we must also insure that our conduct in the enforcement of law and order on college campuses is worthy of the respect of the entire citizenry. The campus is not a privileged sanctuary and law-breaking in any form should not be condoned. Enforcement of the law on the campus must be vigorous, yet never tainted with excessive force or the venting of emotions unworthy of a professional police officer.

Just as we call on college administrators to unite and accept their responsibility of restoring order on their campuses, we, too, in the event of their failure, must perform our duty in strict observance of the rule of law we swore to uphold.

INDEX

To find the names of members of organizations and their boards and councils, signers of statements, discussion leaders, and speakers (as well as their affiliations and topics), please consult the following entries:

Committee for Independent Political Action; New Politics, National Conference for; Socialist Scholars; and Students for a Democratic Society

CRESTWOOD BOOKS, Inc. Distributor
P. O. Box 2096, Arlington, Va. 22202

Kindly rush the following number of copies of books checked.

TEACHERS OF DESTRUCTION by Alice Widener.
( ) Single copy $3; ( ) 3 for $8 ; ( ) 5 for $13.

REVOLUTIONARY ACTIONS IN RETROSPECT - And What To Do
Now compiled by Bruce Alger, including a DICTIONARY OF
DOUBLE TALK (Communese) by Roy Colby.

( ) Single copy 95¢; ( ) 3 for $2; ( ) 5 for $3.

BOTH of the above books -
( ) $3.95; ( ) 3 of both for $9; ( ) 5 of both for $14.

HOW WE PROSPER UNDER FREEDOM, a "short course" in Free-
Choice Economics, by W. T. Hackett and Dr. Emerson P. Schmidt.

( ) Single copy $2.25; ( ) 3 for $5.

Payment of $_____ is enclosed. My check is made payable to CITI-
ZENS EVALUATION INSTITUTE. I understand you pay shipping
charges when payment is enclosed. Write for other quantity prices.

NAME _____
                                      Please Print
NAME OF COMPANY_____

ADDRESS_____

CITY_____

STATE_____   ZIP_____

If you wish books sent to your list, simply add to the multiple copy
price, 35¢ per copy for TEACHERS OF DESTRUCTION; 24¢ each for
REVOLUTIONARY ACTIONS IN RETROSPECT - And What To Do
Now (or 40¢ for both); and 24¢ each for HOW WE PROSPER UNDER
FREEDOM. We pay all addressing, handling, packaging, postage and
shipping charges. (Please include Zip codes in your list.)

The CITIZENS EVALUATION INSTITUTE, sponsor and publisher of TEACHERS OF DESTRUCTION; REVOLUTIONARY ACTIONS IN RETROSPECT - And What To Do Now, (including a DICTIONARY OF DOUBLE TALK) and HOW WE PROSPER UNDER FREEDOM, has arranged with Crestwood Books, Inc. to be the distributor for them. Send orders directly to Crestwood for fast service - but make checks payable to CITIZENS EVALUATION INSTITUTE.

THE CITIZENS EVALUATION INSTITUTE

is a non-profit educational corporation. Gifts to further its work are tax-deductible. For further information write:

CITIZENS EVALUATION INSTITUTE
Education for Freedom Foundation
62 Ben Franklin
Washington, D.C. 20044